Elite • 188

Napoleonic Heavy Cavalry & Dragoon Tactics

PHILIP J. HAYTHORNTHWAITE

ILLUSTRATED BY ADAM HOOK
Series editor Martin Windrow

First published in Great Britain in 2013 by Osprey Publishing,
PO Box 883, Oxford, OX1 9PL, UK
1385 Broadway, 5th Floor, New York, NY 10018, USA
Email: info@ospreypublishing.com

Osprey Publishing is an imprint of Bloomsbury Publishing Plc

Transferred to digital print on demand 2016

First published 2013
2nd impression 2014

 Printed and bound in Great Britain

A CIP catalogue record for this book is available from the British Library

Print ISBN: 978 1 84908 710 0
PDF eBook ISBN: 978 1 84908 711 7
ePub ebook ISBN: 978 1 78200 940 5

Editorial by Martin Windrow
Index by Zoe Ross
Typeset in Sabon and Myriad Pro
Originated by PDQ Media, Bungay, UK

Osprey Publishing is supporting the Woodland Trust, the UK's leading
woodland conservation charity, by funding the dedication of trees.

www.ospreypublishing.com

EDITOR'S NOTE

Because this text includes material quoted from a wide range of historical
sources not specifically listed in the bibliography, the author has provided a
list of numbered source references; these will be found at the end of the
text on page 63.

Unless specifically credited otherwise, all illustrations in the text are from
the author's collection.

ARTIST'S NOTE

Readers may care to note that the original paintings from which the colour
plates in this book were prepared are available for private sale. All
reproduction copyright whatsoever is retained by the Publishers.
All enquiries should be addressed to:

Scorpio Paintings, 158 Mill Road, Hailsham, E. Sussex BN27 2SH, UK
scorpiopaintings@btinternet.com

The Publishers regret that they can enter into no correspondence upon
this matter.

CONTENTS

NAPOLEONIC HEAVY CAVALRY & DRAGOON TACTICS

INTRODUCTION: CLASSES OF CAVALRY

The heaviest of cavalry: an Austrian carabinier in the pre-1798 uniform, loaded down with the weight of his cuirass, slung musket and cartridge pouch, and field equipment including a long picket stake. (Print after R. von Ottenfeld)

At the time of the Napoleonic Wars the distinction between heavy and light cavalry in terms of mounts, equipment, weaponry and tactical employment might best be represented by the armoured cuirassier at one extreme, and the lightly-mounted, less disciplined Cossack at the other. Most cavalry, however, occupied the middle ground between these two, where the distinction was less marked – indeed, the term 'heavy cavalry' was not often used at the time.

The traditional difference between heavy and light cavalry had begun to change by the early 18th century. Originally the classification was defined by the horseman's equipment, the heaviest cavalryman being the cuirassier – the descendant of the medieval knight. In the 17th-century usage of the term, this was a trooper largely encased in armour from head to knee, while the light cavalry were those wearing a minimum of protection, normally a helmet and breast- and back-plates. The demise of the fully-armoured man was largely the result of the weight of his equipment, this being 'exceedingly troublesome to both man and horse', according to Sir James Turner's 1683 manual *Pallas Armata*. George Monck's 1671 *Observations upon Military and Political Affairs* also identified another constant problem: 'There are not many Countries that do afford Horses fit for the Service of Cuirassiers.'

Excluding some lighter-armed troops, who often emanated from particular geographical areas, by the early 18th century the distinction between heavy and light cavalry had become blurred enough that most regiments could be described simply as 'Horse', though the nomenclature could be confusing; until the end of the 17th century, for example, French regiments of 'Horse' were often called *cavalerie légère* simply because they no longer wore the heavy armour of the previous era.

The evolution of 'Dragoons' and 'Horse'

Another class of mounted troops originated in the 17th century: 'dragoons', essentially mounted infantry who rode into battle and fought dismounted with firearms. Initially they were regarded simply as infantry – Turner stated that 'their service is on foot, and is no other than that of Musketeers' – and thus they received only the poorest horses, intended solely for transport and not for action. Nevertheless, dragoons could be used as cavalry, and could even charge (as did Okey's regiment at Naseby in 1645), and their status altered. In Britain, for example, it was ordered in 1684 that dragoons were to rank with infantry in garrison but with the cavalry when in the field; in France, from 1689, dragoons were classed as cavalry except during sieges, when they reverted to infantry. By the mid 18th century dragoons were regarded generally as cavalry, though in some armies they retained the ability to fight on foot, and were usually armed with muskets as well as swords.

As the numbers of specialist light cavalry increased from the mid 18th century onwards the status of the dragoons continued to evolve, so that they came to be regarded as 'heavy' almost by default, to distinguish them from the genuine light troops. The classification was sometimes unclear; even during Napoleon's reign French dragoons were sometimes described as *'cavalerie légère'* merely to distinguish them from the heaviest part-armoured troopers. As the term 'dragoon' came to be applied more widely, in some

BELOW LEFT
A late 18th-century trooper of a French regiment of *Cavalerie*, the arm of service that from 1803 would provide the first 12 regiments of *Cuirassiers*. Note the cavalry musket carried with its butt in a saddle 'boot' below the right pistol holster. (Print by Guichon after Hyppolite Bellangé)

BELOW
Captain Packe and Major Fenwick of the Royal Horse Guards, drawn in 1805; the characteristic appearance of British heavy cavalry uniform and equipment of the early part of the Napoleonic Wars is emphasized here by the caricatured treatment. (Note particularly the huge protective boots.) They appear to carry a variation of the 1796 pattern heavy cavalry sabre, not the basket-hilted *Pallasch* used by this regiment at a later date. (Print by Robert Dighton Jr)

cases the distinction between them and 'Horse' ceased to exist. This was the case in Britain; principally because dragoons were cheaper to maintain. In 1746 the three senior regiments of Horse (after the Royal Horse Guards, which remained a separate classification) were converted to dragoons, being given the title 'Dragoon Guards' to compensate for this loss of status, and in 1788 the remaining four regiments of Horse were converted similarly. They officially remained heavy cavalry, but without the original full dragoon function, and the same applied to the existing and subsequent dragoon regiments that had been formed in the late 17th century.

'LIGHTENING' THE CAVALRY

In the later 18th century there occurred a gradual 'lightening' of cavalry regiments. Shortly after the conclusion of the Seven Years' War in 1763, for example, the French army included 32 regiments of *Cavalerie* ('Horse'), 17 of *Dragons* and three of *Hussards*, excluding the household regiments of the *Maison du Roi*. By 1780 this composition changed to 24 regiments of *Cavalerie*, 24 of *Dragons* and 17 of light cavalry, plus two 'brigades' of *Carabiniers*. In 1803 the term *Cavalerie* was abandoned: the 12 senior regiments became *Cuirassiers*, the heaviest of the heavy cavalry; six more were converted to dragoons, and the remaining regiments were disbanded. At the same time the number of dragoon regiments increased to 30, while the light regiments numbered 34. When the two carabinier regiments are included, this produced a ratio of about 18 per cent heavy regiments, 38 per cent dragoons, and 43 per cent light horse (though a percentage breakdown in terms of regiments rather than numbers is not always conclusive, since lighter regiments commonly had a larger establishment than heavy units).

In the Austrian army, in 1792 there were 11 heavy regiments (cuirassiers and carabiniers), seven each of dragoons and *chevauxlégers* (literally, 'light horse'), and 11 of light cavalry (hussars and *uhlans* – lancers). That the dragoons were not regarded as proper heavy cavalry is shown by the merger in 1798 of dragoon and chevauxléger regiments into a new category, 'light dragoons', only for them to be divided again in 1802. From that date until 1813 Austria maintained an establishment of eight cuirassier regiments, six each of dragoons and chevauxlégers, 12 of hussars and three of uhlans. The same process happened in Russia: the 13 line cuirassier regiments were reduced to six in 1803, but increased again to ten by 1812, while the 11 dragoon regiments of 1803 had increased to 36 by 1812.

This 'lightening' of cavalry was especially marked in the Prussian army, which in 1806 included 13 cuirassier or equivalent regiments, 14 of dragoons, and the equivalent of 12 light regiments (of unequal size). In terms of numbers of squadrons rather than regiments, some 25 per cent of the cavalry were heavy and 31 per cent dragoons. For the 1808–14 period there were (including the Guard) only five cuirassier or equivalent regiments, seven of dragoons (increased to nine in 1815), seven of hussars (increased to 13), and four of uhlans (increased to nine). All the *Landwehr* cavalry, an important resource in the 1813–15 campaigns, was exclusively light. Separate regulations for Prussian heavy and light cavalry were issued in 1796 – one for cuirassiers and dragoons, and another for hussars and 'Bosniaks' (lance-armed light horse), though by the issue of the 1812 regulations there was just one regulation for all types of cavalry.

Distinctions were not universal even in the earlier part of the period: for example, the British regulations of 1796 made no distinction between heavy and light cavalry. Indeed, the Duke of Wellington declared that essentially there should be no difference: 'Our cavalry ought to be the best, that is to say, cavalry of the line, because, in point of fact, when the time comes, they must be so employed, be they dressed and armed how they may'. All, he wrote, should be equally capable of performing 'outpost' duty and of serving 'in line' on the battlefield.[1]

It was not only tactical considerations that led to the maintenance of the heaviest regiments: prestige was also a factor. Heavy regiments were the senior units in virtually every army, and in most armies that maintained an

---

1 For this and all other source notes, see page 63.

Austrian cuirassier officer (right) and his groom in the 1798 uniform, the trooper wearing undress uniform with a forage cap. The officers' saddle covers were of black lambskin, contrasting with the troopers' white covers – yet another feature to make officers quickly recognizable in battle. Assuming the height of the officer to be 5ft 8in, his horse stands a good 15 hands high. (Print after R. von Ottenfeld)

imperial or royal bodyguard the senior regiments were heavy cavalry. Although bodyguard corps were sometimes expanded to incorporate light troops, the closest elements of a sovereign's lifeguard were almost always heavy – for example the Prussian Garde du Corps, Russian Lifeguard, and British Household Cavalry. There were exceptions: Austria never maintained a 'guard' in the sense of other European states, and the emperor's ceremonial mounted bodyguard – the Hungarian Noble Guard – was, as appropriate for that nation, equipped as hussars. Probably the most famous of Napoleon's Imperial Guard cavalry regiments were the light Chasseurs à Cheval, but equally significant was the Guard's original heavy regiment, the Grenadiers à Cheval (see Osprey Men-at-Arms 444 & 456).

MOUNTS

An important factor in the tactical consideration of heavy and light cavalry was the size and power of the cavalryman's mount. In the 18th century especially it was believed that troops mounted on the largest horses would always overthrow those on lighter mounts, and tactics were formulated accordingly. The heaviest cavalry on the largest horses were deployed to charge in a solid mass that would overpower an enemy by sheer impact, whereas the lighter cavalry were expected to move at a more rapid rate and in looser order. This doctrine would evolve as other factors came to be acknowledged as of at least equal significance to mere weight, but to a considerable extent the distinction remained.

A **USE OF THE SABRE: USAGRE, 25 MAY 1811**

For this plate, demonstrating the contrasting ways of using the heavy cavalry sabre, we have chosen to depict one of the rare occasions on which correspondingly-numbered regiments engaged each other: the units shown are the French *4e Dragons* and the British 4th (Queen's Own) Dragoons.

This action during the Peninsular War exemplified how a charge mounted at the correct moment could be devastating. The French commander, Gen Marie-Victor Latour-Maubourg, was ordered by Marshal Soult to turn back pursuing Allied cavalry, and sent his two dragoon divisions to cross a bridge at Usagre to discover their exact location. The leading two regiments of Bron's brigade, the *4e* and *20e Dragons*, had crossed the bridge and were being followed by the third, the *26e Dragons*, when they were attacked from behind a concealing crest by the British MajGen William Lumley, who timed the unexpected charge of his cavalry to perfection. The 4th (Queen's Own) charged Bron directly in front, the 3rd Dragoon Guards in the flank, while Spanish and Portuguese squadrons supported. The leading French regiments were driven back upon the third in total confusion; unable to escape over the constricted bridge, they dispersed along the river bank and were defeated in detail. Though he dismounted part of his second brigade to open fire, Latour-Maubourg was unable materially to assist his troops on the far bank.

The plate illustrates contrasting methods of attack and defence with cutting and thrusting weapons, both when mounted and involving a dismounted trooper. Although the French casualties at Usagre were disproportionately heavy,

the action was quoted as demonstrating the relative qualities of the French and British sabre designs: 'A remark was made at the time by those who were engaged… Only about one third of the French who were struck down … were killed outright; while, on the part of the English, the proportion of killed was much greater than that of the wounded, a circumstance from which it was reasonably inferred that the French sabre was a more destructive weapon than that of our cavalry. The swords of the latter were bad enough for cutting with the edge, but for giving point they were almost quite useless, while those of the French were admirably adapted for pointing, and altogether a far superior weapon'.[37] French losses were about 40 killed and perhaps 200 wounded, but the British loss was probably too low to provide a reliable statistical base: Lumley described the action as 'almost bloodless on our part'.

(1) Downward cut executed with maximum force by British trooper standing in his stirrups; the Frenchman defends with a semi-upright blade, hoping to deflect the blow.

(2) Thrust by the French rider; the British dragoon adopts the standard defence with blade horizontal, in hope of deflecting the blow.

(3) Thrust at a dismounted opponent; again, the British dragoon employs a horizontal guard. This image is copied from a print published by Thomas Kelly, showing the dismounted Samuel Godley of the 2nd Life Guards (who was nicknamed 'Marquis of Granby' because of his bald pate) protecting himself at Waterloo. He not only survived but overcame the cuirassier, and rode off with his horse.

The need to provide suitable mounts for the heaviest regiments could impose restrictions on the very creation of such troops. The requisite size of horse is exemplified by the practice applied by the French (where possible). The unit of measurement was the 'hand'; conventionally, a 'hand' was 4 inches, measured from the bottom of the hoof when the leg was upright to the top of the wither; thus a horse of 15.2 hands measures 62in or 157.5cm. For cuirassiers, mounts were 15.1 hands and above; for dragoons, 15 to 15.1; for chasseurs and hussars, 14.3 to 15; for chevau-légers, 14.1 to 14.3 hands. This presumed that suitable mounts would always be available, but this was not always the case; Napoleon, for example, found it necessary to remount some of his cavalry on captured Prussian and Saxon horses after his victory in 1806, these being superior to their existing mounts.

The bodyguard function of senior heavy cavalry regiments: this illustration shows Gen Eugène de Beauharnais (left), Viceroy of Italy and commander of IV Corps of the Grande Armée, sleeping in the field during the 1812 Russian campaign, watched over by a soldier of the Italian Guards of Honour.
(Print after Albrecht Adam)

The ideal mount for heavy cavalry was probably similar to that in Sir Robert Wilson's description of Russian cavalry: 'The heavy Russian horses are matchless for a union of size, strength, activity and hardiness; whilst formed with the bulk of the British cart-horse, they have so much blood as never to be coarse, and withal are so supple as naturally to adapt themselves to the manège'. He stated that after a march of 700 miles at 35 miles per day, 'they appeared not only in excellent comparative order, but in such high condition, that the regular garrisons of any capital in Europe could not present a finer cavalry parade'.[2]

Larger horses were not only sometimes difficult to obtain, but were more expensive and required more fodder. Napoleon made this point concerning his brother Jerome's Westphalian army in a letter to his foreign minister Jean-Baptiste de Champagny in November 1810:

I have told the king, over and over again, that he ought not to have cuirassier regiments, because that branch of the service costs too much, and the native horses are not adapted for it; that besides, it suited me better to have lancers, and light cavalry, which would be more useful to me, and that, in short, this would have been an immense economy; that the King of Westphalia has taken no notice of this advice – that he is playing at soldiers, and raising regiments of every kind … that I will not have cuirassiers…[3]

Trooper of the Saxon *Leib-Kürassiere-Garde*, 1812, riding one of the heavy 'warmblood' horses for which Saxony was well known. He is wearing a typical 'Germanic' style of heavy cavalry uniform including a blackened cuirass. His weapons are a *Pallasch* sword, a pair of saddle pistols, and a carbine carried hooked to the outer of his two crossbelts, with its muzzle thrust into a small 'boot' hanging below the holster. The inner crossbelt supported the cartridge pouch. (Print after Alexander Sauerweid)

In some armies the difference between the mounts of light and heavy regiments was not so great. In British service there was some attempt to regulate the size of horses; in 1796, for example, it was ordered that dragoon guards and dragoons should be mounted on horses 'not under fifteen and a half hands high', but in practice the difference was not always so marked. In 1813 we find that the majority of mounts of the 2nd Dragoons (heavy) and 10th Hussars (light) were 15–15½ hands, though the former regiment had a larger proportion of 16-hands horses and the latter of 14½ hands; and when the 7th Light Dragoons disposed of surplus mounts in 1814, sizes ranged from 14 to over 15 hands. (For fuller details on the mounts of the British heavy cavalry, see Men-at-Arms 130, *Wellington's Heavy Cavalry*.)

The provision of suitable horses was frequently a problem, as Wellington commented in 1813. He stated that three-year-old horses were unfit for active service and that it was more economical to pay more for a five-year-old, 'the age at which we prefer them here'; failing which, 'there remains then only to draft the five and six year old horses from the regiments on the home establishment… But if this is done, care must be taken that the regiments on the home service do not send us out their old and worn out horses, as they did upon a former occasion, of which there is one instance of the whole remount of one regiment dying in consequence of one day's work'.[4] That this was not an exaggeration is suggested by a comment from an officer of the 14th Light Dragoons in July 1809, in which he complained that a remount of 61 horses – almost cart-horses – had come from the commissariat, 'chiefly Horses that have been *cast* in England as being unserviceable for the *Heavy Dragoons!*'[5]

While the difficulty of finding suitable horses could inhibit the formation and maintenance of the heaviest cavalry, many commentators remarked on the power of the heavier mounts. A light cavalry officer, William Hay, observed the charge of the Union Brigade at Waterloo at close hand:

They came down the slope … like a torrent, shaking the very earth, and sweeping everything before them … the heavy brigade from their weight went over [the infantry] and through them … it struck me with astonishment, nor had I till then, notwithstanding my experience as a cavalry officer, ever considered what a great difference there was in the charge of a light and heavy dragoon regiment, from the weight and power of the horses and men.[6]

Other factors, however, could be crucial. An incident said to exemplify the advantage of the weight of the heavier horse occurred at Genappe on 17 June 1815, during the course of Wellington's retreat from Quatre Bras to Waterloo. The main street of the town was blocked by French lancers in close formation, supported by skirmishers, and when the British 7th Hussars were sent against them they were unable to penetrate the phalanx of lances and were thrown back in disorder; one of their officers declared that they might as well have tried to charge a house. The Earl of Uxbridge then ordered up his heaviest cavalry, the 1st Life Guards, who routed the French. It was claimed that this was because of the power of their heavier mounts; however, it appears that when they saw the 7th Hussars retiring the French began to pursue, and thus lost the advantage of being tightly packed in a narrow street, becoming vulnerable by being in open order. One commentator dismissed the victory in terms of the weight of horses, because 'cavalry, to be either light or strong, must be mounted on horses fully equal to the weight they have to carry ... heavy cavalry and heavy infantry are terms for heavy heads to amuse themselves with; in modern war, cavalry and infantry, if they are to be strong, must be light also'.[7]

EQUIPMENT

Sabres

Tactical considerations determined the cavalryman's arms and equipment. The primary weapon of most cavalry was the sabre, especially for the heavier regiments, whose use of firearms was limited. In general, light cavalry tended to carry curved sabres designed to execute a slash, whereas most heavier cavalry used heavier, straight-bladed weapons. Sometimes equipped with a 'basket' guard to protect the hand, some were of a type known by the German term *Pallasch* – a heavy, broad-bladed weapon with an edge designed to execute a cut; an alternative type also usually had a heavy guard, but with a narrower, pointed blade designed for a thrust.

A brass-hilted *Pallasch*, the characteristic style of heavy cavalry sword with a protective basket hilt including, in this case, a thumb-guard.

There was considerable discussion regarding the most effective variety of sabre. Many commentators favoured the thrusting weapon, such as Maurice de Saxe, whose writings were respected long after his death in 1750; he advocated that swords should have blunt edges to compel the soldier to execute only the thrust. This was also the opinion of the influential Prussian general Karl Emanuel von Warnery, who explained that by raising the arm to execute a cut the swordsman might expose his body to the enemy's blow.

Prussian dragoons skirmishing; the short-barrelled carbine was supported on the bridle arm for firing. This print shows the dragoons in the light blue coatee (*Kollet*), though for active service the longer frock-coat (*Litewka*) was often preferred. The firing soldier has his ramrod hanging vertically from one of his chest buttons.

The ornate metal helmet of a trooper of the elite Westphalian Garde du Corps, 1807–13; the decorative crest or mane is missing from this example. (Museum für Deutsche Geschichte, East Berlin; photo courtesy Digby Smith)

RIGHT A classic heavy cavalry headdress of 'Germanic' style: a Württemberg leather *Raupenhelm* ('crested helmet'). The thick, hardened leather of the skull and the raised comb, strengthened with metal edging, was as protective as a metal helmet against sword cuts while being lighter to wear. However, that protection was less than complete in either case.

In some armies, however, the cut was preferred, as explained by the British 1796 manual that discouraged the use of the thrust against cavalry: 'For if the *point* is parried, the adversary's blade gets within your guard, which is not to be recovered in time … the point should seldom or never be given in the attack, but principally confined to the pursuit, when it can be applied with effect and without risk… Against infantry, the point may be used with as much effect as the edge and with the same degree of security' (*Rules and Regulations for the Sword Exercise of Cavalry*, 1796). Adaptations could be made, however: the British 1796 heavy cavalry sabre was designed so exclusively for the cut that originally it had a 'hatchet' point; but in 1815, seemingly at the prospect of facing armoured cuirassiers for the first time, the blades were ground to a point so that a thrust was more practical.

The cavalry trooper was taught almost to fence on horseback, with specific cuts and guards against enemies to right and left, at his own level and below him (as when engaging infantry), while protecting his own head, body, arms and thighs. The British manual quoted above stated that all movement should come from the shoulder and wrist, executed with a straight arm, so as not to expose the forearm to the enemy's cut by bending the elbow. Although the thrust was potentially the most lethal blow, in combat the principal object was to disable the enemy, not necessarily to kill him, and it was thought that the cut also had an effect on the enemy's morale. The British light dragoon George Farmer remarked of French casualties caused by British sabres: 'The appearance presented by these mangled wretches was hideous… as far as appearances can be said to operate in rendering men timid, or the reverse, the wounded among the French were thus far more revolting than the wounded among ourselves'.[8] (Statistics concerning casualties are not always conclusive, as in the case of the action at Usagre, described in the commentary to Plate A, which was cited as exemplifying the difference between thrusting and cutting weapons.)

This Austrian equipment worn from *c.* 1805 is typical of the 'German' style of cuirass consisting of a breastplate only, supported by a waist belt and crossed rear straps from the shoulders. An officer's helmet and armour are shown at left, a trooper's at right. The former had a gilded helmet comb embossed at the sides with a lion motif, and their cuirass had brass edging and a central brass 'arrowhead' dart pointing downwards from the top edge. (Print after R. von Ottenfeld)

Firearms

Heavy cavalry used firearms very much less than the light cavalry, and since the heaviest troops were not expected to skirmish these weapons were not regarded as important. Indeed, in the heaviest French regiments, carbines ('musketoons') were not even issued until 1812, and were greeted by one cuirassier officer with incredulity: Aymar de Gonneville remarked that their issue was 'quite senseless. On horseback and wearing the cuirass, it was quite impossible to make use of them'.[9] Similarly, in 1813 the British cavalry commander Stapleton Cotton ordered that carbines be withdrawn from the Household cavalry regiments (save six per troop, presumably for the use of sentries), on the premise that they were never expected to skirmish and that the horses had enough weight to carry already. One Austrian commentator dismissed cavalry firearms altogether, in case they discouraged the troops from rushing at the enemy with the sabre.

Pistols were also of limited tactical use, though carried by almost all cavalrymen; there are accounts of pistols being used in a mêlée, but there was probably much truth in the British comment that 'We never saw a pistol made use of except to shoot a glandered [diseased] horse'.[10] Only under extreme circumstances was the pistol of real value, as in one encounter at Dresden when rain prevented infantry from firing and made the ground too heavy to permit cavalry to move quickly. French cuirassiers broke an Austrian infantry formation by firing their pistols (which must have been kept dry in their holsters) until sufficient gaps appeared for the cavalry to ride in and use their sabres.

Armour

The cavalry's principal defence was the helmet, and many of the heavier regiments wore metal or leather constructions that afforded a degree of protection. Even these were vulnerable to a sabre-stroke, however, which led Marshal Marmont to state that a shako reinforced with wood on the crown would be more effective (and presumably less arduous to wear).

The use of body-armour had declined almost to extinction by the end of the 18th century. Its weight inhibited the ability to skirmish, and imposed difficulties in finding horses of sufficient strength to carry men so burdened, so the cuirass was generally restricted to armies large enough to accommodate regiments reserved exclusively as a striking-force on the battlefield. (Marmont in fact declared that armoured cavalry should be reserved for acting against infantry, when the armour might offer some protection from musketry.)

Of the principal European armies, only that of Austria retained a force of armoured cuirassiers throughout the Revolutionary and Napoleonic Wars, and even so, that arm was reduced by one-third by 1802. Both Prussia and Russia had heavy cavalry that were styled 'cuirassiers', but this reflected tradition rather than equipment. Having abolished the cuirass in 1790, Prussia only re-adopted it in 1814–15, while Russia only began to issue body armour in 1812. Other armies had too few cuirassier regiments to employ them as a 'shock' element *en masse*, unless they were intended to serve alongside cuirassiers of allied armies (as was the case with the one Duchy of Warsaw and the two Westphalian regiments, for example). Others had only token armoured regiments, like Spain, which formed its single regiment in 1810, utilizing cuirasses captured from the French 13e Cuirassiers.

French cuirassiers, showing the 'whole' cuirass with both breast- and back-plates. The latter was made thinner and lighter than the breastplate, but would still turn a sword-blow in a mêlée. (Print after R. de la Nézière)

 PRUSSIAN CUIRASSIER SQUADRON IN LINE, c.1813

This plate provides a visual impression of the size of a squadron drawn up in a two-rank line, though the frontage would vary according to the numbers of men present. (We show about 48 troopers in each of the two ranks; upon the reconstruction of the Prussian army after the defeat of 1806, squadron strength was set at 125 men.) In this system, only the *Rittmeister* squadron commander (**R**) was positioned in front of the line. In the centre of the front rank were the *Premierleutnant* senior lieutenant (**PL**) and standard-bearer (**S**), and another lieutenant (**L**) and a trumpeter (**T**) rode on the right flank. Both officers in the front rank were 'covered' by an *Unteroffizier* NCO (**U**) in the second rank. The supernumerary rank in the rear was formed by other lieutenants (**L**) and NCOs (**U**), including behind the right flank a lieutenant and the *Wachtmeister* squadron sergeant-major (**W**).

There were at this period only four Prussian *Kürassiere* regiments: 1st Silesian, 2nd East Prussian, 3rd Garde du Corps

and 4th Brandenburg. Subsequently the Garde du Corps was removed from the numbered sequence; the Brandenburg was renumbered as the 3rd; and a new 4th (Magdeburg) Regiment was created, from squadrons of the other three and from Saxon personnel incorporated into the Prussian army after Napoleon's defeat. The dress uniform was a white coatee (*Kollet*), but for active service a dark blue frock-coat (*Litewka*) was preferred. The helmet was of leather with a high comb, but, despite the title of the arm, cuirasses had been withdrawn in 1790 and were not reintroduced until April 1814.

(**Inset**) An important aspect of command and control was the trumpeter, since orders transmitted by trumpet-call were more audible than verbal commands, especially in combat. This vignette shows an officer and trumpeter of Austrian cuirassiers; trumpeters of cuirassier regiments, as in France, were unarmoured, recalling their original non-combatant function, and in many armies they rode grey horses so as to be easily identifiable on the field of battle.

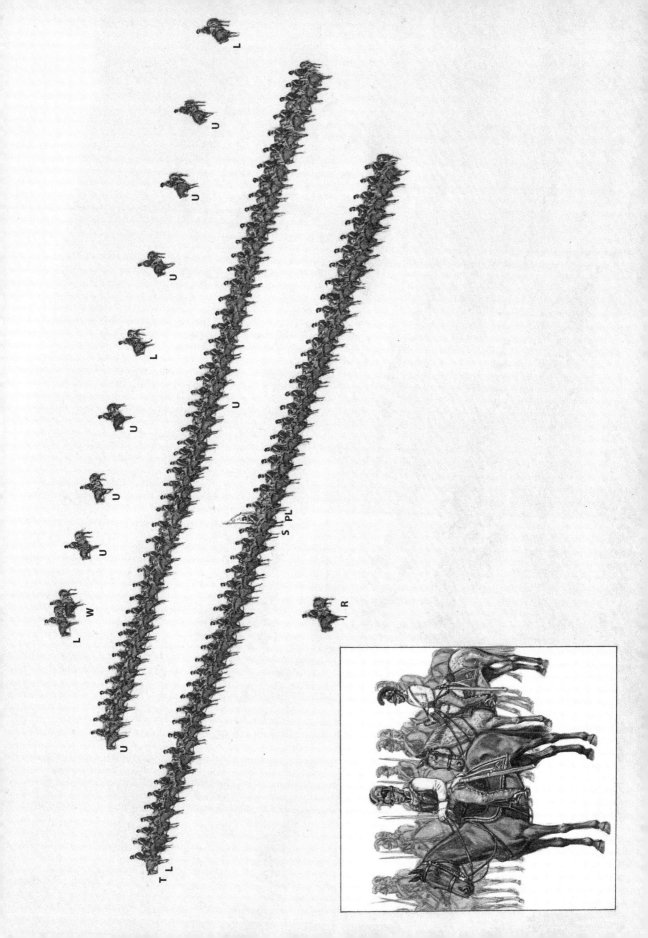

A mannequin displaying the uniform and helmet of a French officer of *Cuirassiers*, c.1810, with what seems to be a trooper's cuirass – the officer's model had a deeply incised line forming a margin inside a row of gilded rivet-heads around the edges. The helmet chin strap and the shoulder straps of the armour are faced with brass scales to protect them from sword cuts. The iron helmet has a brass comb embossed for strength, fitted with a horsehair mane; here its upswept front, together with the downswept angle of the peak, shows the neo-Grecian 'Minerva' style fashionable from about 1808 onwards. Field status (i.e. from major's rank up) is indicated by the tall white feather plume and the short, thick silver bullion fringe on the paired epaulettes. The prominent cuirass-lining of bullion-laced red cloth saved the uniform from being chafed by the edge of the metal. (Musée de l'Empéri, courtesy the late M. Raoul Brunon)

It was in France that the cuirassier arm was most prominent. Initially only a single regiment was so equipped, the 8e Cavalerie (known as Cavalerie-Cuirassiers, ex-Cuirassiers du Roi). In 1802–03 the existing Cavalerie regiments were equipped with cuirasses, forming initially the 1er–12e Cuirassiers, their number rising subsequently to 15 regiments. Additionally, in 1810 the two Carabinier regiments were also equipped with cuirasses.

An example of an army insufficiently strong to maintain a dedicated armoured element, Britain used virtually no body-armour for its heavy cavalry. Its only experience was in the Netherlands in 1794, when the Royal Horse Guards received cuirasses, and iron skull-caps to be worn under the hat; but these were found unduly cumbersome and were returned to store, and a recommendation by the Board of General Officers in May 1796 that all cavalry should be equipped with cuirasses was ignored. The evaluation that the cuirass was an unnecessary burden was not unique; for the 1812 Russian campaign, for example, one of the two Saxon armoured regiments, the Zastrow Cuirassiers, did use its armour, but the other, the Garde du Corps, left theirs in Warsaw at the outset of the campaign, protecting themselves in action by wearing their cloaks rolled and slung diagonally across the body – a very common practice.

There were two styles of body-armour: a 'whole' cuirass comprising a reinforced breastplate and a lighter back-plate, as favoured by the French, and another consisting of the front plate alone, used by some German regiments. There were conflicting opinions on the merits of the two patterns. The Austrian commentator mentioned previously dismissed cuirasses entirely: 'Let the cuirasses of cavalry decorate the arsenals… Why load [men] with armour which does but incommode them. The rear-plate is only useful to guard cowards, who turn their backs on the enemy, and thus render themselves unworthy of protection; and the breastplate is little advantageous if the General does not expose the cavalry to attacks until prepared to repel them'.[11]

Nevertheless, the cuirass did have some protective value, and at longer range it could turn a musket ball. The first French cuirasses were supposed to stop three balls at 30 paces, but when numbers failed this test the requirement was reduced to one shot at longer range. Knowledge of the protective qualities could cause a variation in tactical practice; in the 1815 campaign, for example, British infantry were ordered to fire at the horses rather than their riders, which led Rees Gronow of the 1st Foot Guards to lament the fate of the animals more than that of the men.

Antoine de Marbot recounted an incident that demonstrated the properties of the two styles of cuirass, when at Eckmühl in April 1809 French and Austrian cuirassiers crashed together, while the accompanying light cavalry drew off to the flanks to avoid being caught up in the fight.

The cuirassiers advanced rapidly upon each other, and became one immense mêlée… Courage, tenacity and strength were well matched, but the defensive arms were unequal, for the Austrian cuirasses only covered them in front, and gave no protection to the back in a crowd. In this way, the French troopers who, having double cuirasses and no fear of being wounded from behind had only to think of thrusting, were able to give point to the enemy's backs, and slew a great many of them with small loss to themselves... [When the Austrians wheeled about to withdraw] the fight became a butchery, as our cuirassiers pursued the enemy... This fight settled a question which had long been debated, as to the necessity of double cuirasses, for the proportion of Austrians wounded and killed amounted respectively to eight and thirteen for one Frenchman.[12]

A further item of protective equipment used by heavy cavalry was a consequence of the knee-to-knee charge formation: the long boots worn to prevent the legs being crushed. Some thought them more an encumbrance than a protection, as Marbot observed of a dismounted cuirassier officer at Eckmühl who was unable to run fast enough to escape the enemy – he was killed in the act of pulling off his boots.

ORGANIZATION

Unlike infantry regiments, which might comprise a number of autonomous battalions, cavalry regiments were usually complete in themselves, organized in a manner dictated as much by tactical as administrative considerations. In almost all armies the standard regimental sub-unit was the squadron, usually divided into two troops or companies.

The squadron was the basic tactical unit that could operate independently on the battlefield, and which underpinned the system of manoeuvre. Establishments varied: for example, in 1807 French cuirassier regiments each comprised five squadrons of two companies each, each company numbering three officers and 102 other ranks; with a regimental staff of seven officers and 20 other ranks, this produced a regimental establishment of 1,040 other ranks. At the same time, the equivalent Austrian cuirassier regiment comprised six squadrons of 135 men each, with a number of supplementary dismounted troopers who in wartime provided the cadre for a reserve squadron of 143 men. The reason that squadron establishments were similar in most armies was the fact that any number of men greater than 200 were difficult to control and unwieldy to manoeuvre. Troops or companies, too, were usually subdivided, with varied terminology: in the Prussian system, for example, each troop comprised two platoons or *Zügen*, while the British regulations used the terms 'half-squadron' (for troop) and 'division' (for a quarter-squadron, or half-troop).

Regimental establishments were rarely attained on campaign, and were generally governed by the number of available mounts rather than of riders. The size of regiments varied greatly, from those described above to very much smaller. For example, the British heavy regiments at Waterloo in 1815 had an average strength of 479 all ranks (excluding the Household regiments, each of which had only two squadrons present), and at Salamanca in 1812 only 358 all ranks. Because of the differing sizes of regiments, it was advocated at the time that the most reliable method of estimating the strength of a force was to gauge it in terms of squadrons, not regiments.

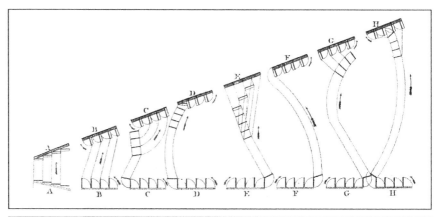

Brtish instruction for a regiment of four squadrons changing direction by about 45 degrees, while riding (from bottom to top) in line. The eight troops are here lettered A to H. Each troop of say 100–120 men first splits into four sub-divisions; these manoeuvre in column, then form a new line at a diagonal angle to the original facing. This evolution would require about 30 separate verbal commands.

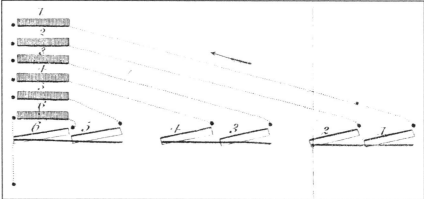

British instruction for a regiment of three squadrons to form column from line preparatory to withdrawing (enemy to the bottom in this case). The six numbered troops defile to form a column-of-troops facing in the opposite direction from the original facing.

TRAINING, AND FORMATIONS

Training and discipline were of paramount importance, as stated by the future Duke of Wellington in 1804:

> The formation and discipline of a body of cavalry are very difficult and tedious, and require great experience and patience in the persons who attempt it… At the same time nothing can be more useful in the day of battle than a body of disciplined cavalry, nothing can be more expensive, and nothing more useless than a body of regular cavalry … insufficiently disciplined.[13]

The consequences of insufficient training were exemplified by the experience of Aymar de Gonneville, whose 15e Cuirassiers, organized at Hamburg in 1813, included many novices. On first ordering his men to draw their sabres, 'the blades issued from the scabbards fairly well together, but the glitter and the noise that they made frightened the horses so much that they started off like a flight of pigeons, jumping about in all directions and getting rid of their riders, most of whom threw themselves on the ground' – this caused their commander such anguish that he thought that the only way he could avoid disgrace would be to get himself killed![14] It was also the case that whereas new recruits could be introduced into a battalion of infantry without impairing its ability to operate, 'a few half-formed dragoons, a few unbroke horses, will throw a whole line of cavalry into disorder'.[15]

While each army had its own system of manoeuvre the essence was fairly standard, but often of a complexity that required intensive training. In the

British system, for example, the change of facing of a regiment in line to a new position at some 45 degrees from its original facing, which might appear a fairly simple manoeuvre, required about 30 separate verbal commands. The detailed, step-by-step specification of manoeuvres was intended to ensure the maintenance of good order, though it is likely that the more complicated evolutions were reserved for the parade ground. In infantry service there is evidence that only the basic manoeuvres and changes of formation were required on the field of battle, and it is likely that the same applied to the cavalry.

For example, when commenting on manoeuvring by threes, in his edition of the Württemberg general Count Friedrich Wilhelm von Bismarck's *Lectures on the Tactics of Cavalry* (1827), Maj North Ludlow Beamish, an officer of the British 4th Dragoon Guards, wrote that the drill produced only complicated movements 'which, like Chinese puzzles, only engross time and labour to the unprofitable end of forming useless combinations'. Some clue about which manoeuvres were deemed essential may be gathered from

An Austrian cuirassier officer sits a couple of horse-lengths in front of his men drawn up in a two-rank line. Behind him to his right, at the extreme right of this picture, is his trumpeter, distinguishable in a mêlée by his red helmet crest, grey horse, and lack of a cuirass. It was important that officers could immediately locate their trumpeters, to speed the tranmission of orders. (Print after R. von Ottenfeld)

Four squadrons change their direction of facing by a relatively simpler manoeuvre than that shown at the top of page 20: the eight troops simply wheel and march in echelon.
Key: (A) = original line;
(F) = the wheel at an angle by troops;
(G) = the advance in echelon;
(B) = the troops wheel into their new line.

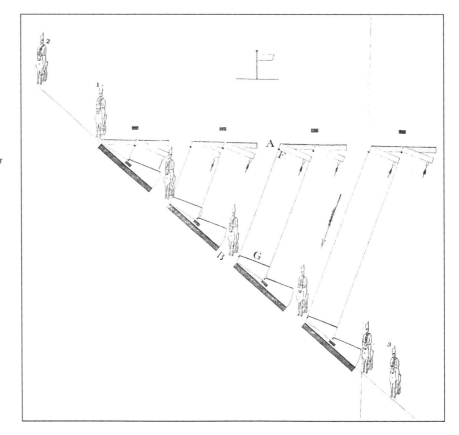

abbreviated sets of manoeuvre instructions. The British regulations of 1796 contain 108 sets of manoeuvres, whereas the official manual issued in 1803 for Yeomanry and Volunteer cavalry – whose members would have less time to learn their drill – was restricted to 37 principal manoeuvres. One of the unofficial 'elucidations' of the regulations (*The Light-Horse Drill*, London, 1802) compresses the 374 pages of the official version into just 37 (albeit rather more tightly set) pages.

Formations

Although each army had its own drill and system of manoeuvre, the basic tenets were generally similar. For movement outside of combat the standard formation was the column; this was much easier to keep in order during movement than a line, into which it was relatively simple to deploy. Even when action was imminent commanders employed the column, which better concealed the strength of the body from the view of the enemy. There were several varieties of column, from the column of march (three or four riders abreast, for travelling on roads), to columns with a frontage rising from half-troop to troop or even squadron, with the appropriate diminishing depth.

For action, the preferred formation was the line, though the number of ranks was a matter of some discussion. An earlier opinion held that three ranks were preferable; this provided additional 'weight' in the shock of the charge, while the third rank assisted in impelling the others onwards. In this theory a two-deep line was only advocated as a way for a weaker unit to match the frontage of its opponents, to prevent the enemy from assailing a shorter line in its flank. The disadvantage of a third rank, however, was that

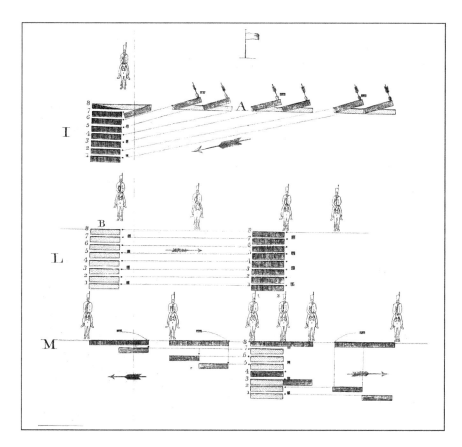

Change of position by four squadrons. From line (A) the regiment forms a column-of-troops (I) upon the troop at the left. (B) the column advances to (L), then the troops defile to their right, taking up a new position in column. They then deploy into a line (M), taking up positions on either flank of the central troop, here numbered 8.

a fallen horse in the front rank could cause more disorder than it would to a two-deep line.

There were variations on this theory: for example, a writer in the *British Military Library or Journal* (1798) advocated three or even four ranks when attacking cavalry, when there would be no musketry to bring down the front rank. Again, the Prussian 1796 regulations did specify three ranks for the charge, but the third rank was not to follow the others – it was to draw off into a body on either wing, to attack the enemy's flank if the opportunity arose.

Generally the two-deep line became the preferred formation, as exemplified in changes to the Austrian regulations. Those of 1784, which were in use at the beginning of the French wars, used a two-deep line for skirmishing but three ranks for other manoeuvres; the two-rank line later became standard, and was confirmed by the reforms of 1805 and the 1806 regulations. There were varied distances between ranks and files; the British manual, for example, specified that the usual distance between ranks should be sufficient to permit the easy wheeling of mounts, with 'close order' being approximately half the length of a horse (about 3ft 6in, or 1.07m), measured from the tail of the front-rank horse to the head of the rear-rank mount. With 'close files' the rider's boot-tops touched those of his neighbours; with 'loose files' (the usual distance) boot-tops were 6in apart, sufficient for the preservation of order at all speeds; and with 'open files', a full horse-breadth separated the riders.

When a squadron was drawn up in line, officers and NCOs were distributed to maximize command and control. The numbers of such personnel varied between armies, as did their positions; some armies integrated officers in the front rank while others, like the French,

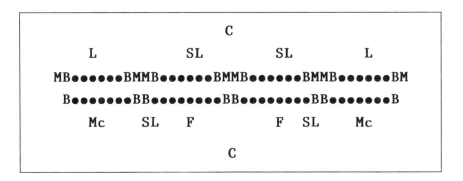

had officers (at least initially) riding ahead of the front rank. The British practice was described in their manual: one officer should be posted at each flank of the front rank, each 'covered' by a corporal (i.e. with a corporal riding immediately behind him); an officer should carry the squadron standard in the centre of the front rank, covered by a corporal (this officer presumably exercising a conventional command function when the standard was not carried, as was usually the case on campaign); the commanding officer was to ride one horse-length in front of the standard; three sergeants were spaced along the front rank, on the right of each of the four 'divisions' except the right one (where a front-rank officer rode), each sergeant being covered by a corporal or trooper; and supernumerary

FRENCH CUIRASSIER SQUADRON IN COLUMN

This presents a visual approximation of the amount of ground occupied by a squadron of French cuirassiers drawn up in 'column-of-divisions', i.e. with each half-company division arrayed in two ranks, one division following the other. The frontage was wider than most minor roads of the period, so whenever cavalry passed along them wide margins of ground on each side would usually be churned up by their hoofs, especially in wet weather.

Precise dimensions would vary according to circumstances; here we show approximately 12 men per rank, so about 108 all ranks in this squadron, but the frontage was officially 24m exclusive of the officers or NCOs riding on the flanks of the front ranks. The gap between the rear of one division and the front of that following was also 24m, i.e. equal to the frontage of each division, thus permitting the divisions to pivot into line at right-angles to the original facing. Although the *lieutenants* and *sous-lieutenants*, (L) and (SL), rode in front of the front rank of each division, the squadron's senior officers – *capitaines* (C) commanding the two companies – were positioned on opposite flanks of the front rank of the two central divisions. The corporals and sergeants – *brigadiers* and *maréchaux-des-logis*, (B) and (M) – rode on the flanks of each front rank. The quartermaster-corporals (*fourriers*, F); the company sergeant-majors (*maréchaux-des-logis chef*, Mc); and the warrant officer (*adjutant-major*, AM) all rode behind the rear ranks of the divisions.

(Inset) The squadron standard-bearer (a senior NCO), with his coverers or escort. The standards were significant as symbols of regimental identity, and of the connection between the regiment and the sovereign in whose name they were bestowed. Although in most cases standards were not actually carried on campaign, they could be an important element of command and control, marking the location where a squadron might rally. In Napoleon's armies initially each squadron carried a standard, but their use declined, until it was ordered that only one 'Eagle' per regiment should be taken on campaign, as in instructions to the army in Germany in 1809. A decree of December 1811 restricted the granting of an Eagle to cavalry regiments of no less than 600 horses, in effect only one per regiment, to be carried by the 1st Squadron. (At least three French cuirassier regiments lost their Eagle and standard in the Russian campaign of 1812.)

A similar practice was followed in Prussian service. After the reorganization of 1806, standards were only permitted for cuirassiers and dragoons, initially one per squadron, but from October 1811 it was ordered that only one per regiment should be taken on campaign, and it was not until 1814 that light cavalry were permitted standards at all. The evidence for British practice is less clear-cut, but it seems likely that if standards were taken on campaign in the Peninsula they were left at rear depots in Lisbon; we read that those of the 4th Dragoon Guards were 'left aboard the Admiral's ship'. Writing of the Union Brigade – 1st, 2nd and 6th Dragoons – in the 1815 campaign, Col Clarke Kennedy of the 1st (Royals) told William Siborne: 'Please to recollect that none of the brigade took their standards into the field, they were left at home by order.' The 1st Life Guards did take their standards across the Channel in April 1815, but they were soon sent back to the depot.

or 'serrefile' (file-closing) officers and NCOs were to form a partial third rank, two horse-lengths behind the second rank, to keep that rank in order. Troop quartermasters were also positioned in this third rank, specifically to direct movements.

The regulations took account of the effect of casualties: if officers were lost they were to be replaced in the line by sergeants, sergeants by corporals, and corporals by 'intelligent men'. If any command personnel left their positions in the line for any other reason their coverers also moved up to replace them, to maintain the integrity of the formation. The French cavalry officer A.F. de Brack, who wrote one of the most valuable commentaries on cavalry service, stated that the duty of *serrefiles* was to force their way into the second rank when the order to charge was given, preventing any cowards from hanging back, and that once the mêlée had begun their duty as file-closers was ended.

Dimensions of formations were dependent largely upon the number of men present. In the French system, for example, a 'column-of-divisions' involved each 'division' (half-troop/half-company) formed in two ranks with a frontage officially of 24 metres (excluding officers and NCOs on the flanks), so that a squadron of two troops/companies would include four such two-rank formations one behind the other (as illustrated in Plate C), with a gap officially of 24 metres between the rear of one division and the front rank of the succeeding division. This spacing would thus allow each division to pivot through 90 degrees to deploy from column into line. Officers and NCOs were posted either on the flanks of the first rank of each division, or between the divisions. A 'column-of-troops/companies' had double the frontage and half the depth. This emphasizes the fact that although the squadron was the primary tactical element, each troop/company and each 'division' was a manoeuvre element with its own command echelon.

Pace, and endurance

The pace at which manoeuvres were conducted varied according to circumstance, but in general speed was sacrificed to the maintenance of good order. The British regulations exemplified best practice:

> The *Walk! Trot!* and *Gallop!* are the three natural paces, and of each of these there are different degrees of quickness; but at which ever of them the squadron is conducted, the slowest moving horses at that pace must be attended to, otherwise different kinds of motion will exist at the same time in the squadron, and tend to disunite it... Though single horses or small bodies may instantaneously change from one pace to another; yet a squadron or a number of bodies will move with more ease and uniformity, when such transitions are made gradually through the different paces, as from a *Walk* to a *Slow Trot! Quick Trot! Slow Gallop! Quick Gallop!* and vice versa... All alterations of pace must be made as much as possible at the same instant, by each separate body that composes a line or column... In general, all changes of position and manoeuvres should be made at the *Trot* or *Gallop*, according to circumstances, beginning gently to avoid hurry, and ending gently to avoid confusion... Great bodies, consistent with perfect order, cannot move with the same degree of rapidity as smaller ones, and therefore an allowance proportionable to their extent must be made in conducting them, whether in line or column, and this only the eye, practice, and attention can determine.[16]

One of the leading contemporary authorities, Ralph Adye, stated that the 'usual rate of marching' of cavalry was 17 miles in six hours, 'but this may be extended to 21, or even 28 miles in that time', and this could be exceeded over short periods if the circumstances required and the nature of the terrain allowed it. For precise movements in the field, Adye stated that 'military horses *walk* about 400 yards in 4½ minutes, *trot* the same distance in 2 minutes 3 seconds, and *gallop* it in about 1 minute'.[17]

(Left) French dragoon in Egypt, 1798; and (right) a dragoon mounted. In each case note the long dragoon musket carried on the right side of the saddle, butt downwards. (Prints after Rozat de Mandres, and Martinet)

SKIRMISHING, AND DRAGOONS

Although heavy cavalry was not as suited for skirmishing as were the light regiments, it did perform part of this service. To some extent the effectiveness of cavalry skirmishers was influenced by the nature of their principal firearm, the carbine. Short-barrelled weapons like the Austrian 1798 model or the British Paget pattern (16in barrel) had a very limited range, but were easier to manage when firing from horseback. Longer-barrelled weapons were more effective, although one commentator stated that the French 'chasseur carbine' – presumably the *An IX* pattern with a barrel length of 75.8cm (29.8in) – had a range at least twice as long as was necessary, implying that cavalry skirmishing should be carried out at short range.

Varied importance was placed upon cavalry skirmishing. For example, in Austrian service mounted fire had attained some prominence, notably against

A British squadron in line (enemy to the top).
Key: Co = squadron commander; O = subaltern officers; S = sergeants; C = corporals; Q = quartermaster-sergeant. In this schematic, the number of troopers shown is unrealistically small.

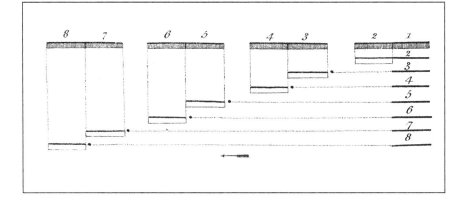

Co

O●●●●●●S●●●●●●●SO●●●●●●●S●●●●●●O
S●●●●●●C●●●●●●CS●●●●●●●C●●●●●●S
S   Q   S   Q   O

British instruction for deployment of a regiment of four squadrons from column-of-troops into line to the left (enemy to the top) – see Plate D. Troop 1 stands fast; the others defile left, then turn to their right, and advance into line successively, next to one another.

D BRITISH REGIMENT DEPLOYING FROM COLUMN INTO LINE

This gives an impression of the extent of ground occupied by a British dragoon regiment of four squadrons, c.1812, when deploying into line from 'column-of-troops'. Each squadron comprised two troops. These were usually numbered from 1 to 8, running from front to rear when in column and from right to left when in line, so that when deployed into line, No.1 troop was on the extreme right flank, No.8 on the extreme left. Deployment from column-of-troops was reasonably simple, as shown; the leading troop in the column stood fast, the succeeding troops turning to left (as here) or right, riding in file parallel to the intended regimental line, and then wheeling right (as here) or left to take up the intended position in the line.

The plate shows Nos.1 and 2 Troops of 1st Squadron and Nos.3 and 4 Troops of 2nd Squadron already formed into line; No.5 Troop has wheeled from double file into (a therefore shorter) line and is riding forward, and No.6 has just wheeled and is about to ride forward; Nos.7 and 8 Troops are still in double file and riding towards their wheeling positions. A similar deployment could be executed by the leading troop standing fast and the succeeding troops deploying alternately to left and right simultaneously, so that the original leading troop became the centre of the new line.

For clarity in this small-scale schematic treatment the gap between the two ranks of each squadron in line is shown as wide enough to allow the easy wheeling of horses; on the battlefield the regiment would in fact form before action in 'close order', i.e. with a gap between ranks officially of only 3ft

6in (1.07m) measured from the tails of the front rank of horses to the heads of the second rank. The squadrons in line are drawn up separated by manoeuvring gaps. No precise measurement of frontage was stated in the regulations, this being dependent upon the number of men present. Squadrons maintained a fairly uniform strength on campaign, as it was important that sub-units had an equal composition, even if this required the transfer of men from one troop to another.

Only the regimental commander (**RC**) and squadron commanders (**CO**) were positioned in advance of the line, with their trumpeters (**T**). The positions within the squadrons were as shown in the diagram on this page (**top**). Subaltern officers rode on the flanks of the front rank, covered by two of the sergeants in the rear rank, and with sergeants and troop quartermaster-sergeants in the *serrefile* rank two horse-lengths behind the rear rank. Other sergeants and corporals were distributed among the troopers along the ranks. On parade a standard was positioned in the centre of each squadron's front rank, but these were not usually carried on campaign.

(**Inset**) One service of heavy cavalry is sometimes overlooked: duty as sentries or vedettes. Although the heaviest cavalry were not expected to skirmish, all were able to post sentries, and even to perform the 'outpost' duties for which the light regiments were more suited. The troops shown are British dragoons post-1812, wearing their cloaks as in bad weather, and making (fairly rare) use of their carbines. Units that did not carry carbines – such as French cuirassiers before 1812 – would use their pistols for such duties.

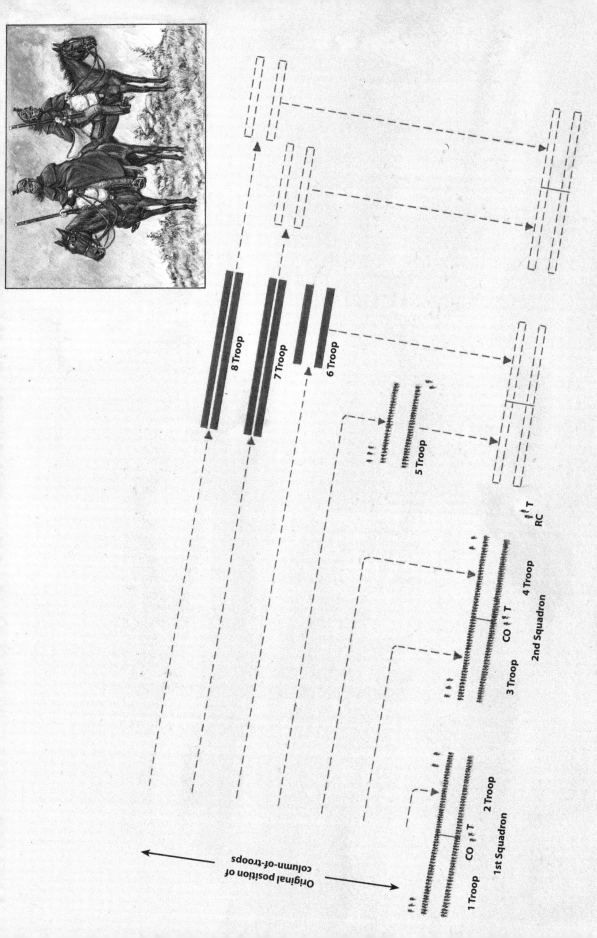

1 Troop   CO   T   2 Troop

1st Squadron

Original position of
column-of-troops

3 Troop   CO   T   4 Troop

2nd Squadron

RC   T

5 Troop

8 Troop

7 Troop

6 Troop

ENEMY

the Turks; heavy cavalry as well as hussars originally carried the 1770 carbine, and in 1792 six men in every squadron were issued with a rifled carbine, the 1789 *Cavallerie-Stutzen*. Subsequently the Austrian dragoons and chevauxlégers carried carbines, with 16 rifles per squadron, while cuirassiers and uhlans had eight rifles and eight carbines per squadron. Subsequently their use was not so much encouraged, shock action with the sabre being more highly regarded.

In the Prussian cavalry, each cuirassier squadron initially had ten men armed with rifled carbines, and dragoon squadrons 12, positioned on the flanks of a line. However, the 1812 regulations provided for 48 'flankers' in each squadron, and 12 rifle-armed marksmen. In action the designated 'flankers' formed a firing line in front of the main body; cuirassiers, dragoons and uhlans generally used pistols and the others carbines. The rifle-armed men were positioned 20 to 30 paces behind the skirmish line, selecting specific targets with their more accurate weapons, and protected by the flankers when they dismounted to take better aim. Because the heaviest troops were not best suited for skirmishing, from 1813 units of volunteer Jägers might be attached to the heavy regiments; these were usually young men of some substance who enrolled as a patriotic duty, and who were trained and equipped as light cavalry to add an extra dimension to the capabilities of the heavy regiments.

Some heavy cavalry seem to have become quite proficient in skirmishing and similar light cavalry-style duties, especially those units that were not of the very heaviest nature. The experience of the British 1st (Royal) Dragoons seems to have been an example of this: it was stated that in the Peninsula they shared outpost duty with the light cavalry, to the extent that they were nicknamed 'Whitbread's Hussars' (from their black horses, resembling the dray-horses of that famous brewery). Conversely, shortly before the battle of Vittoria in 1813 the sight of Household cavalry mounting outposts prompted some derision: 'Although the men and horses looked gigantic, and bore a fine appearance, still the idea of out-post duty for the heavy cavalry caused much merriment in the ranks'.[17] This was despite the fact that the 1796 heavy cavalry carbine was a well-made weapon with a 26in barrel.

Following the issue of carbines even the heaviest of cavalry, the French cuirassiers, seem to have practiced skirmishing despite their lack of suitability for that role. An account of coming under their fire was recorded by the British artillery officer Cavalié Mercer, who recalled how at Waterloo '...the cuirassiers led the second attack ... sending up a cloud of skirmishers, who galled us terribly by a fire of carbines and pistols at scarcely 40 yards from our front'. To prevent his gunners wasting shot by firing at these individual targets Mercer rode up and down in front of his guns, though this attracted the cuirassiers' fire:

> The tall blue gentlemen ... immediately made a target of me, and commenced a very deliberate practice, to show us what very bad shots they were... One fellow certainly made me flinch, but it was a miss; so I shook my finger at him, and called him *coquin* &c. The rogue grinned as he reloaded, and again took aim... Whenever I turned, the muzzle of his infernal carbine still followed me. At length it went bang, and whizz came the ball close to the back of my neck, and at the same instant down dropped the leading driver of one of my guns (Miller), into whose forehead the cursed missile had

A trooper of the Empress's Dragoons of Napoleon's Imperial Guard, with equipment that recalls the original infantry function: a musket, a cartridge pouch slung from the left shoulder, and the waist belt extended to form another shoulder belt to support the sabre above the ground when dismounted. (Print by Lacoste after Eugène Lami)

penetrated. The column now once more mounted the plateau, and these popping gentry wheeled off right and left to clear the ground for their charge.[18]

Conversely, the unsuitability of the heaviest cavalry as skirmishers was exemplified by an incident in the 1813 German campaign when a French cuirassier regiment, advancing in column, was assailed by Cossacks along their flank and rear. The Cossacks fired and thrust their lances at the column until the cuirassiers were in some confusion, unable to respond effectively until finally some files on the flanks turned outwards and began to shoot back, but they were only saved by the arrival of reinforcements.

French Dragoons

The French dragoons, however, were a different case, and offer as near an example as any to the original concept of dragoon service. As well as having the ability to fight on foot they became a mainstay of Napoleon's battlefield cavalry arm, though the latter ability was not always appreciated. Marshal Marmont, for example, stated that dragoons should revert to their original calling as mobile infantry, with horses selected merely to carry them into action and too small to serve in the proper cavalry. The alternative, he declared, was that dragoon colonels would try to convert their regiments into conventional cavalry, with the consequence that they would be neither good infantry nor effective cavalrymen.

Even Napoleon wrote something similar in August 1806 when advising his brother Joseph on the disposition of his forces in Naples. He advocated that, rather than scattering his forces over the kingdom (where many were engaged in anti-guerrilla duties), Joseph should concentrate his dragoons: 'Give them four or six pieces of light artillery… Treat them as infantry, and organize them so as to move rapidly… By keeping them under the orders of

---

E

FRENCH DRAGOONS SKIRMISHING

To some degree cavalry skirmishers operated in a similar way to those of the infantry, some aspects of which, performed by French dragoons, are illustrated here (more details of the techniques of skirmishing will be found in the forthcoming companion title, ELI 196 *Napoleonic Light Cavalry Tactics*). Unlike the cavalry of some other nations the French did not have designated skirmishers; all could undertake the task, especially in the case of the dragoons. This imaginary scene from the Peninsular War shows skirmishers deployed both on foot and mounted, to delay an Allied advance from the direction of the bottom of the plate towards the French-occupied Spanish village on the hill in the background. (In reality, it is perhaps unlikely that dismounted and mounted men would operate together in quite such close proximity.)

(**1**) As with infantry skirmishers, cavalrymen seem to have operated in pairs perhaps 8 to 10 yards apart, which enabled one man always to be loaded to cover his comrade while he reloaded. The skirmish line was usually deployed in two ranks, with the front-rank men firing; the rear rank could thus advance through the gaps and take their turn in shooting, once the original firers had reloaded.

(**2**) Officers and perhaps senior NCOs could remain mounted; even in the *Dragons à Pied* the officers retained their horses.

(**3**) The horses of the dismounted men would be held perhaps 100 yards behind the skirmish line, out of the enemy's range; the provision of these horse-holders would thus reduce the notional combat strength of each unit by at least 25 per cent.

(**4**) For skirmishing when mounted the same basic rules applied. The dragoons are spaced perhaps 5 yards apart.

(**5**) Where possible, as illustrated, it was prudent to retain a mounted reserve some distance behind the firing line, which could be used to support the skirmishers or to cover their withdrawal.

(**Insets**) French dragoon skirmishers. The mounted man (**1**) shows the technique for firing from the saddle; it was recommended that this should be to the right of the horse's head so as not to risk the animal panicking if hit by sparks from the lock. Loading when mounted presented a difficulty if the ramrod were dropped; remedies included carrying the ramrod on a strap attached to the belt, or having the ramrod fixed to the carbine by a swivel. The dismounted dragoon (**2**) is a member of the *Dragons à Pied*, with a mixture of cavalry and infantry equipment: infantry gaiters, cartridge box and knapsack, and with the waist-belt lengthened for wear over the shoulder. The sword was frequently not carried by the foot dragoons, but all were equipped with bayonets.

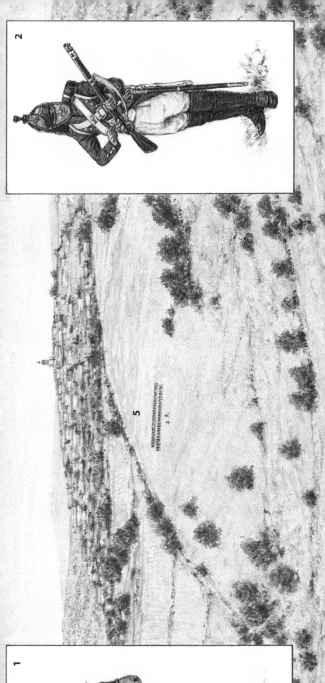

ENEMY

a single commander, who would put them every day through their foot exercises, you would make them into excellent infantry'.[19]

Although the performance of the dragoon regiments in the early campaigns of the Empire was somewhat patchy, in the Peninsula they proved highly effective, and were virtually the only heavier cavalry deployed there by the French. They proved adept in all duties, from the battlefield charge to escorts, patrols and anti-guerrilla work, and when withdrawn from Spain to assist Napoleon in 1813–14 they proved battle-hardened and efficient – the most effective of the diminished cavalry in the army that he was having to rebuild once again after the losses in Germany.

One factor that contributed to the effectiveness of Napoleon's dragoons was their principal firearm, the dragoon musket, which was only about 10cm shorter than that of the infantry (the *An IX-XIII* pattern had a barrel length of 1.28m/ 50.4 inches). Indeed, it was also carried by some infantry skirmishers, who found its length more handy for their task. The consequence was described by Jonathan Leach, who encountered them in the Peninsula:

The French dragoons ... were armed during the Peninsular war with a long fusee [sic], which could throw a ball as far as the musket of an infantry soldier... our dragoons, on the contrary, both light and heavy, were armed with a little pop-gun of a carbine. The consequence of this was, that when bodies of cavalry met at a distance from their infantry, the French dragoons often dismounted where the country was intersected and woody, and shot at our dragoons at a distance which rendered our short carbines almost useless... In the French army, one man was left in charge of three or four horses, out of reach of fire, whilst the dismounted dragoons or chasseurs became efficient light infantry, and acted as such if their own infantry were not up.[20]

French dragoons employed as heavy battlefield cavalry: a trooper of the *16e Dragons* at the charge. He wears the simpler single-breasted green *surtout* coatee of this branch, with pink regimental facings and lining, and grey riding overalls buttoned up the outside. This regiment served in the Peninsula, and was among those later withdrawn from Spain to rebuild Napoleon's badly weakened cavalry for the 1814 French campaign, in which they formed an invaluable resource. (Print after Rozat des Mandres)

An example of the versatility of such troops occurred at Corunna in 1809, when the French cavalry general Armand Lahoussaye, commanding three dragoon regiments, endeavoured to halt the advance of Edward Paget's Reserve Division against the French left flank. The terrain was unsuited for conventional cavalry manoeuvres, being intersected with walls and gullies, and Lahoussaye's attempts to charge were so futile that Paget's infantry did not even need to form square, but drove them off with rolling volleys. Finding cavalry tactics impractical, Lahoussaye dismounted his 27e Dragons and dispersed them as *tirailleurs* in a skirmish screen; although they were too few to stop the British advance, the advantages of troops who could dismount and fight effectively on foot were obvious.

The troops who came nearest to Marmont's concept of dragoons were Napoleon's Dragons à Pied, units of dragoons assembled to serve solely on foot. This was not primarily a tactical experiment but arose from one of the periodic shortages of horses, to utilize troops for whom no mounts were available. The first such formation was organized at the camp at Boulogne for the projected invasion of England: five brigades, organized in two divisions, with infantry equipment (including drummers in infantry style), but ordered to carry their horse-furniture with them in the baggage train so that they could be mounted on captured horses once the invasion gained a foothold. For the 1805 campaign four provisional regiments were formed, each of two battalions of two companies each, from the dismounted squadrons of almost all the dragoon regiments. The system was not without problems – some veterans were assigned to the dismounted units, while recruits were given horses – but the units proved useful for escort duty and could serve quite effectively as infantry. Similar provisional formations served in Italy and in the 1806 campaign, where the dismounted men received horses when sufficient were captured from the Prussians and Saxons. At the conclusion of campaigning such dismounted units were disbanded, the men returning to their original regiments, but their service on foot had demonstrated the versatility of Napoleon's dragoons.

Dismounted service was not restricted entirely to the French army; dragoons of other armies also served on foot at times, for example in the Russian army in 1812, but such expedients were again born of shortage of horses rather than of deliberate tactical doctrine.

Dragons à Pied skirmishing. Retaining their cavalry helmets, sabres and uniforms, they carry infantry knapsacks and wear infantry gaiters. The trumpeter at right carries an infantry drum. (Print after Horace Vernet)

HIGHER FORMATIONS

The tactical employment of cavalry was influenced significantly by the organization adopted in the field, and vice versa. Generally cavalry was organized in brigades of two or more regiments (four was about the most that could operate effectively as a brigade), although individual units might be detached and functioned perfectly well on their own.

The separation between light and heavy regiments was common, most notably in armies possessing sufficient mounted troops for particular roles to be assigned to whole formations of these categories. However, light and heavy regiments might serve in the same brigade, which was not necessarily a disadvantage if the 'heavies' were able to perform a wide spectrum of duties. (In the British army in the Peninsula, for example, for a considerable period the 'heavy' 1st Dragoons was brigaded first with the 14th Light Dragoons and subsequently with the 12th.) The association of light with heavy cavalry units was sometimes a tactical decision, exemplified by the divisions of Napoleon's reserve cavalry in the 1812 campaign; since cuirassiers were not suited for scouting and skirmishing, each division of cuirassiers and carabiniers also included a regiment of *chevau-légers lanciers*, light troops attached specifically to perform these duties.

The disposition of cavalry brigades varied between armies and with circumstances. Two or more brigades could be combined to form a division, though this might be as much for organizational as for tactical reasons. There were two principal methods of utilizing cavalry: in their own separate mounted formations, or as 'corps cavalry', in which one or more brigades could be attached to a *corps d'armée* to perform the mounted duties required by that all-arms formation. Light cavalry was most suited for this role, with the heavier regiments concentrated into their own divisions to maximize their offensive potential. Cavalry divisions might be attached at corps level as much as an offensive as a support arm, but practice varied. The Austrians,

F
DEPLOYMENT OF A BRIGADE

This illustrates a notional brigade deployment immediately prior to engagement, as might have been the case with the British Household Brigade at Waterloo. The plate is not in true scale, and it is unlikely that this precise arrangement would have been seen in practice, but it does show several modes of movement and array.

(1) In the centre of the front line is a regiment halted in line, four squadrons with the usual manoeuvring gaps between them; in the case of the Household Brigade, this would be the 1st (King's) Dragoon Guards.

(2, 2) On either flank a regiment is coming into line alongside the King's: respectively, the 1st and 2nd Life Guards, each of which fielded only two squadrons in 1815. On the right flank the squadrons of the 1st Life Guards are advancing in column, one directly behind the other; when one comes into line with the King's the following squadron will defile to right or left, march parallel to the front line, then turn to come alongside the first (as on Plate D). On the left flank, the two squadrons of the 2nd Life Guards are advancing in echelon, so that by continuing forwards both will come directly into line.

(3) The fourth regiment – in the case of the Household Brigade, the Royal Horse Guards – is halted several hundred yards to the rear as the reserve. It is shown drawn up in columns, each column with the frontage of a single troop; alternatively all four troops could be arrayed one behind the other, or in an even deeper formation with a half-troop frontage. In all cases sufficient room is left between squadrons, and between lines, to permit manoeuvring without the danger of a retiring or advancing unit carrying confusion into the remainder.

(Inset) This shows one of the specified poses for the charge, as described in the British regulations: 'In the trot and gallop the right hand must be steadied on the right thigh, the point of the sword rather inclined forward – and in the *Charge* the hand is lifted, and the sword carried rather forward and crossways across the head, with the edge outwards'. The trooper shown wears the uniform of the Life Guards for service, c. 1815, with campaign horse-furniture and the plain, single-breasted jacket that replaced the heavily-laced coatee worn for ceremonial duty.

3

2
left

2
right

1

Command echelon: a French general gives orders to the commander of the cuirassier regiment in the background. The general's entourage includes officers in staff and hussar uniforms, and – at right – an escort of dragoons. (Print after C. Wittman)

for example, initially assembled brigades and divisions on a somewhat *ad hoc* basis, and showed an increasing tendency to dilute the cavalry's power by attaching units to protect the flanks of infantry formations, rather than assembling large bodies to execute decisive offensive manoeuvres on the battlefield.

Napoleon – who, unlike many commanders, for years had at his disposal truly awesome numbers of genuine heavy cavalry – adopted the reverse policy. This was exemplified by his organization of the Grande Armée for the 1812 campaign, when he created four independent corps of 'reserve cavalry'. (The term 'reserve' in this instance can be deceptive: it was 'reserve' in the sense of being held back for specific tasks, but did not imply a second-line formation.) Of these four corps, three comprised two heavy divisions, each of three brigades mostly of cuirassiers and carabiniers (one heavy division had two dragoon brigades), plus one light brigade to provide the skirmishing and reconnaissance capability. The fourth corps consisted of one light and one heavy division, assembled from allied contingents. The primary purpose of these reserve corps was to act *en masse* on the battlefield, executing 'shock' action.

Circumstances, however, could frustrate tactical doctrine. Commenting upon the use of cuirassiers in French service, Marbot stated that they were capable of resisting charges and of breaking through enemy formations by virtue of their weight, but not of providing rapid support for the light cavalry advance-guards. He attributed heavy losses in the cuirassier arm in the campaigns of 1809–13 to the despatch of most of the army's dragoons to Spain, so that the cavalry of the field army in central Europe consisted primarily of light cavalry and cuirassiers. As the latter were required to provide support at decisive moments, their horses, which needed more food and less work, were kept in readiness for deployment at short notice throughout the day, every day. This caused such fatigue that many broke down even before going into action – and when they were finally sent in to support the light cavalry, they often arrived too late because of their limited pace.

Such considerations underlined the value of a more flexible form of cavalry, in which nominally 'heavy' regiments were sufficiently versatile to perform a wider range of duties. This factor was inter-related with tactical doctrine; for example, by contrast with Napoleon's practice, the Prussian 1812 regulations integrated cavalry into 'brigade' tactics (a Prussian brigade generally equated to an all-arms division). These saw them held at the rear of the brigade's infantry, with strong forces usually in column behind the flanks, and able to sally forward outside the flanks of the infantry to exploit any success or to engage oncoming enemy cavalry. (See Elite 182, *Prussian Napoleonic Tactics 1792–1815*.)

Leadership was an important element in cavalry tactics, and some generals became especially associated with heavy cavalry. One such was Francois-Etienne Kellermann (1770–1835), Count – later Duke – of Valmy. Arguably his greatest exploit was at Marengo in June 1800, when the charges of his heavy brigade (*2e, 20e* and *21er Cavalerie*) helped to turn the course of the battle. He is remembered for commanding III Cavalry Corps (of cuirassiers, carabiniers and dragoons) at Waterloo in June 1815; but he also led light cavalry on occasion, as at Austerlitz in December 1805. His fame as a cavalry general was somewhat marred by his reputation as an unbridled looter.

THE CHARGE

The power of a huge, decisive charge was well known from the Seven Years' War, when Frederick the Great's heavy regiments sometimes proved devastating. However, there was a widely accepted doctrine that massed cavalry charges should only be launched against infantry already weakened by artillery and musket-fire. This was articulated by, for example, Gen Joseph Rogniat, one of the most distinguished of French military engineers. He wrote that 'cavalry of the line' (heavy cavalry) should be employed in large bodies, being held in reserve until late in a battle when it could be launched against the enemy flank,

The charge: Marshal Joachim Murat and his staff (most of them wearing hussar uniform) leading a regiment of dragoons into action at Jena, October 1806. The charge has progressed to the stage at which the men begin to raise their sabres and cheer, though Murat himself carries only a riding crop. Murat's career revealed many character flaws, but lack of personal courage in battle was not one of them. (Print after F. de Myrbach)

or in forcing an opening through the enemy's line, as soon as the cannon and musketry shall have produced disorder and numerous vacancies among them. It is thus that the movements of the cavalry of the line may secure the victory, at the end of a battle, in the moment when the infantry, fatigued and exhausted by a long contest, presents only an uncertain and ill-directed fire. But if we were to allow it to charge at the commencement of the battle, upon infantry unharmed and firm, it would doubtless be forced back upon the rest of the army, which would be infected with its disorder.

Neveretheless, Rogniat quoted one case that seemed to contradict this conventional wisdom: the success of the Union Brigade against d'Erlon's advance at Waterloo (where Rogniat himself served). He claimed this was as much a consequence of the irresolution of the infantry as of the power of the cavalry: 'One of our columns, dismayed at the mere aspect of this cavalry, fled, and dispersed... [The cavalry] owed its partial success solely to the inexperience of our foot soldiers, who, being but newly formed into battalions, had not, as yet, acquired the unity and *ésprit de corps* which constitutes the strength of the infantry'. A more usual consequence of charging resolute infantry, he stated, was the fate suffered by the massed French cavalry charges at Waterloo, where, having gained a position amidst the Allies, they 'allowed themselves to be almost all killed under a dreadful shower of projectiles rather than abandon it'.[21] Wellington himself described

something like the latter case in his opinion on Napoleon's use of heavy cavalry:

> He gained some of his battles by the use of his cuirassiers as a kind of accelerated infantry, with which, supported by masses of cannon, he was in the habit of seizing important parts in the centre or flanks of his enemy's position, and of occupying such points till his infantry could arrive to relieve them. He tried this manoeuvre at the battle of Waterloo, but failed, because we were not to be frightened away.[22]

There were, however, some instances in which heavy cavalry proved successful against an enemy that was not already wavering. The cuirassier attack against the Russian 'Great Redoubt' at Borodino in September 1812 was a remarkable example, involving the assault of earthworks defended by resolute troops. It was a combined-arms operation involving the infantry of Napoleon's IV Corps and his II and IV Reserve Cavalry Corps, but the horsemen outdistanced the infantry. The cuirassiers of II Reserve Cavalry Corps were driven off (notably with the loss of Gen Auguste de Caulaincourt); but a brigade of IV Cavalry Corps, including the Saxon Garde du Corps and Zastrow Cuirassiers, outflanked the Russian position and overran the earthworks from the rear, the success being consolidated by the arrival of the infantry.

One of the greatest charges was mounted at Eylau in February 1807, which, like the attack on the Borodino redoubt, was a matter of circumstance

A charge in column: French cuirassiers skirt around the 'Great Redoubt' at Borodino, September 1812. In the left foreground an aide kneels beside the body of Gen Auguste de Coulaincourt, shot dead at the commencement of the attack. (Print by Audibon after Raffet)

Cuirassiers penetrate the earthworks of the Great Redoubt, at the climax of one of the most remarkable attacks launched by heavy cavalry during this whole period. (Print after Albrecht Adam)

rather than of premeditated tactical policy. Napoleon had assaulted the Russian line with infantry but had been driven back, and his whole position was in jeopardy from Russian counter-attack. His salvation was Murat's cavalry, which had been intended to deliver a *coup de grâce* once the Russian line had been sufficiently mauled; instead, it had to be sent forward in a defensive attack to stabilize Napoleon's position.

Led by Murat in person, this charge involved largely heavy cavalry: the 2nd Cuirassier and 1st, 2nd and 3rd Dragoon Divisions, followed by the Imperial Guard cavalry – some 80 squadrons numbering about 10,700 men, moving at not much more that a walk due to the state of the snow-covered and muddy ground. The attackers penetrated the Russian line, reorganized, and charged back to their own positions. The price they paid was some 1,500 casualties, or about 15 per cent of those involved; but the massed charge saved the day for Napoleon, and demonstrated that cavalry could be used as a primary striking-force in its own right, and not just as a support arm, or one reserved to complete a victory already half-won by others. However, as Gen Sir Evelyn Wood was to remark on the subject of charging unbroken infantry, a successful outcome was not a recommendation that such tactics should always be employed.

Balancing impetus with control

The exact methods employed to deliver a cavalry charge varied between armies, but some aspects were universal. Principal among these was the necessity of retaining discipline and formation until the moment of contact, even if this required a reduction in speed. Many would have agreed with Wellington's observations on the subject: 'It is impossible to preserve order, and go quick in large bodies. It is equally so to traverse the spaces which the manoeuvre of large bodies requires should be traversed, and keep the horse in a state to do any thing, if the pace is not slow. But the great object of all in the cavalry, and particularly that of the line, is *order*'. He noted the necessity 'to keep the charge, as well as all other movements, at the pace with which, at least, the middling goers, if not the slowest, can keep up'; otherwise, 'The horses are jaded before the moment of exertion arrives, and it becomes impossible for any man to produce the great effect with the cavalry of which it is capable'.[23]

The necessity of maintaining order was obvious – troops meeting the enemy in a dispersed formation would be brushed aside by a more solidly-formed opponent; but even so, some commentators emphasized the advantages of speed. Frederick the Great had written of the need 'to overset the enemy by the furious shocks of our cavalry. By means of this impetuosity, the coward is hurried along, and obliged to do his duty as well as the bravest; no single trooper can be useless. The whole depends upon the *spirit* of the attack'.[24]

Similarly, Marmont was less concerned with preservation of the closest order than with the ability to manoeuvre at speed, believing that it was worth sacrificing a little order for the impetus that cavalry usually needed to succeed, providing that troops were trained to rally after the first shock. Some commented on the psychological effect of the charge at speed, both in heartening the chargers and unnerving the enemy, who might be so alarmed that they would turn about rather than face the impact – indeed, this was one of Frederick's declared objectives. Others advocated a combination of the two: for example, C.J.J. Ardent du Picq, one of the most perceptive commentators of the period after the Napoleonic Wars, stated that cuirassiers should charge at a trot until the enemy broke, and then pursue at a gallop.

Even an advance at a steady pace could be daunting, as recounted by Cavalié Mercer when facing French cuirassiers at Waterloo:

> The spectacle was imposing, and if ever the word sublime was appropriately applied, it might surely be to it. On they came in compact squadrons, one behind the other… Their pace was a slow but steady trot. None of your furious galloping charges was this, but a deliberate advance, at a deliberate pace, as of men resolved to carry their point. They moved in profound silence, and the only sound that could be heard from amidst the incessant roar of battle was the low thundering reverberation of the ground beneath the simultaneous tread of so many horses. [At 50 to 60 yards' range Mercer has his battery open fire:] The effect was terrible. Nearly the whole leading rank fell at once… Still, however, these devoted warriors struggled on, intent only on reaching us. The thing was impossible… The discharge of every gun was followed by a fall of men and horses like that of grass before the mower's scythe.[25]

This was no isolated example; Napoleon's heaviest cavalry, especially in the later campaigns, habitually seem to have charged at a relatively slow pace. Some commentators believed that the very weight of the heavy cavalry fatally inhibited its ability to move quickly; it was stated that the heavy losses suffered at Aspern-Essling in May 1809, when the French cuirassiers moved only at a trot and in column, were due to the fact that they were incapable of doing otherwise. More than one critic of Napoleon's tactics averred that the slow pace was the consequence of a combination of the burden imposed upon horses carrying large, armoured men, and deteriorating standards of

Grenadier à Cheval of the French Imperial Guard, as he might have appeared during Murat's great charge in the snow that stabilized Napoleon's position at Eylau - although that attack was not in fact delivered at a gallop. It was while this regiment, in reserve, were waiting in the saddle under heavy fire that their colonel Gen Louis Lepic is supposed to have reprimanded his men for ducking: 'Heads up, by God! – those are bullets, not turds!' The moment was later immortalized in Detaille's famous painting. (Print after Rozat de Mandres)

G A CHARGE *EN ECHIQUIER*

This plate depicts a charge by a four-squadon regiment of French cuirassiers against Austrian infantry, *c.* 1809. The formation illustrated was a variation of the echelon, styled *en echiquier*, whereby the leading squadrons – (**1**), (**2**) – were separated by about a squadron's frontage (*c.* 60–80 yards), with the succeeding squadrons – (**3**), (**4**) – covering the gaps in the front line checkerboard-fashion. Distances depended upon circumstances, but the second line might be about 100–150 yards behind the first; the gaps between squadrons permitted those of the first line to retire without disordering the second line. When used against infantry, in theory the first line might absorb the enemy's musketry and, if unsuccessful, would be succeeded by the second line, which would fall upon the enemy before they had a chance to recover from the initial clash. This formation was also used when covering a retreat, with lines retiring in turn, covered by those in the rear.

The deployment of each French squadron was fairly standard, in two ranks. The *lieutenants* and *sous-lieutenants* – (**L**), (**SL**) – rode in front of the first rank. Sergeants and corporals (*maréchaux-des-logis* and *brigadiers*) were positioned in the front line on the flanks of each of the two companies, on the flanks of the divisions half-way in towards the centre, and in the centre. The *adjutants-major* warrant officers (**A**) rode a couple of horse-widths out from the flanks of the front rank. Senior NCOs – the *fourriers* quartermaster-corporals and *maréchaux-des-logis-chef* sergeant-majors, (**F**) and (**Mc**) – were spaced along behind the rear rank as *serrefiles*, to exercise control. The two *capitaines* company commanders (**C**) rode in the centre at front and rear of the line, the captain commanding the squadron at the front with his trumpeter (**T**), and the junior captain in the rear. The gap between ranks might be about two horse-lengths, so that members of the second rank had a chance to avoid colliding with falling horses in the first rank. As the pace increased, gaps in the front rank would be filled by men from the second rank, and the *serrefiles* would also move up into the ranks.

(**Inset**) Charging troopers might ride knee-to-knee, actually touching the men to right and left, as in the case of the Austrian cuirassiers depicted here. Immediately before contact the men would stand up in their stirrups, raise their sabres and cheer – actions intended to unnerve the enemy as much as to hearten the troopers.

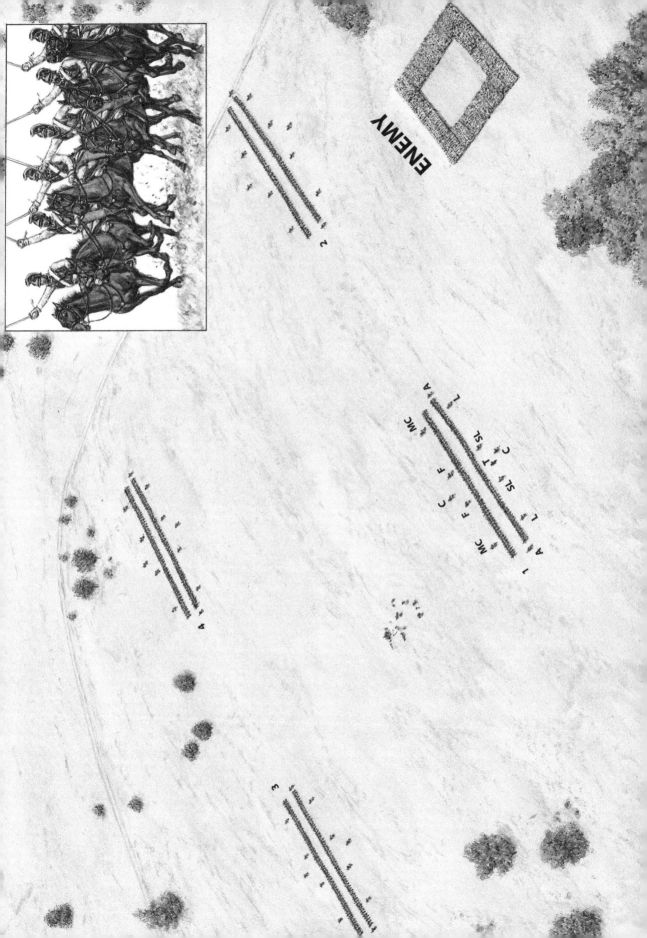

ENEMY

mounts and horsemanship, inhibiting the flexibility and rapid movement exhibited in some earlier campaigns.

Circumstances might also prevent an all-out charge '*à l'outrance*', for example the nature of the terrain, the softness of the ground or the fatigue of the horsemen. Such was the configuration of the ground and the proximity of friendly infantry that the great charge of the Union Brigade at Waterloo, though memorably depicted in Lady Butler's painting 'Scotland For Ever' as a headlong gallop, actually made first contact with d'Erlon's infantry at a trot, at the most, after moving over the crest of the Mont St Jean ridge so near to their target that one witness stated that they 'actually walked over' the column that they first rode down.[26]

TECHNIQUES

The knee-to-knee charge, '*en muraille*' (like a wall), as performed by heavy cavalry, could be executed in such close formation that individual riders might be virtually helpless. Lewis Edward Nolan of Balaclava fame recorded how he rode in such a formation in the Austrian cavalry, packed so tightly that his horse was at times lifted off its feet by the pressure from either side, causing great pain to the rider. This was not exceptional; a British report of 1794 concerning a field day of the Life Guards stated that 'Several accidents happened; one of the horses reared up so high, that he fell backwards upon his rider, who was so dreadfully bruised [sic] that his life is despaired of. Another soldier had his thigh broke, by being jammed between his own horse and that of his comrade'. [27]

Even within a disciplined charge such factors could affect cohesion. There was a tendency for horses to crush in towards the centre, which increased in larger formations; attempts to remedy this could disorganize the line, and close off the gaps left to facilitate manoeuvre. Conversely, there was also a tendency for horses on the extreme flanks to become detached from the main body, again interfering with the manoeuvring gaps; the positioning of officers and NCOs on the flanks of the line was intended to prevent this.

The charge in line, echelon or column

There were several formations in which a charge could be delivered, dependent to some extent upon the nature of the terrain, since enclosed or broken ground was not suited for expansive manoeuvres. Although the principal formation for a charge was the line, in which several squadrons could be arrayed alongside each other with manoeuvring gaps between them, a number of other formations were in fairly common employment.

Among these was the attack in echelon, in which individual squadrons were deployed as in line but staggered, so that the leading squadron would come into action first, succeeded by that on its left or right, with the others following in turn. In theory this method produced a number of successive blows against the enemy which applied increasing pressure until they gave way. It could also be especially effective against infantry, who might expend their fire upon the cavalry's leading element so that the succeeding squadrons might have an uninterrupted run at them. (A variation is shown in Plate G.) It was also useful when withdrawing, with each squadron falling back in turn, protected by that nearest the enemy. Another variation described in the Austrian regulations was to mount a linear attack with additional squadrons in echelon on the flanks, so that while the central contingent occupied the enemy frontally the flanking echelons could swing out and engage the enemy's flanks.

A columnar attack involved squadrons or troops formed directly behind one another. This employed something of the principle of the echelon attack, in that the leading squadron might absorb the fire of the enemy and then disperse, while succeeding squadrons, sheltered from fire as they approached, pressed the charge home before the enemy could reload. Although attacks in column were quite common earlier in the period, it was stated that (in the French service, at least) they came to be used primarily against infantry. This was especially so in the later campaigns, as the calibre of Napoleon's cavalry suffered from the attrition of long campaigning; the column attack was easier for less well-trained or inexperienced men. One of its advantages over the line as a formation for use against infantry in square or close column was that a charge in line would so overlap the flanks of the enemy that only one of the cavalry unit's squadrons could engage. If the squadrons were in column, one after another could come into action – recalling the 17th-century *caracole*, in which successive units advanced, engaged, then withdrew, to be followed by those behind one after another.

Columns, however, were notably vulnerable to flank attacks. Whereas infantry could form a new face relatively easily, this manoeuvre was much more difficult for cavalry, and depended upon the column having sufficient manoeuvring gaps equal to the frontage of the column. A combination of units in column with others following in line was a derivation of a tactic used by Frederick the Great; in the case of the French, units in column on the flanks of a charging line could turn and deploy to meet any attack incoming from the flank.

Light and heavy cavalry might be combined deliberately, notably when skirmishers were used to precede a charge, screening the main body and then withdrawing to the flanks or through gaps in the advancing line. Even heavy cavalry could advance skirmishers under such circumstances, especially in armies in which the difference between heavy and light troops was less marked, as for example in the Prussian army during the 1810–15 period.

Timing

One of the most important features of the charge was its timing, to ensure that the enemy was contacted at maximum impetus, without the horses being 'blown' by having galloped too far. Ideally speed was built up gradually; the British regulations, for example, stated that a unit was to move at a 'brisk trot' until within 250 yards of the enemy, then gallop:

> The word *Charge!* is given when within eighty yards, and the gallop increased as much as the body can bear in good order... At the instant of the shock, the body must be well back; the horse not restrained by the bitt, but determined forward by the spur; rising in the stirrups, and pointing the sword, will always occasion a shake in the squadron... It is in the uniform velocity of the squadron, that its effect consists; the spur as much as the sword tends to overset an opposite enemy; when [the] one has nearly accomplished this end, the other may compleat it [sic]... Regiments and squadrons must be well dressed before they move; horses perfectly straight, and carried on so during the whole attack; files on no account crowding; paces even and determined; horses in hand, and perfect steadiness and attention of every individual.[27]

At Aldenhoven in October 1794, French dragoons, following horse artillery, advance in the foreground in the classic two-rank formation, with a frontage of apparently half a company. (Print after Mozin)

OPPOSITE
The climax of a charge: having got to about 80 paces from the enemy, an Austrian cuirassier officer shouts 'Marsch!', his trumpeter blows the 'Alarm', and the troopers raise their sabres. The uniforms shown here are pre-1798. (Print after R. von Ottenfeld)

Most other regulations prescribed a similar process, with pace increasing from trot to gallop. The Prussian regulations, for example, advocated that two-thirds of the distance to the enemy be covered at a trot, which was then increased to a gallop; 200 paces from the target trumpeters sounded the charge, and at 80 paces the commanding officer raised his sword and ordered the charge, 'Marsch!'; the other officers followed suit, and the pace increased to a fast gallop. The Austrian regulations concurred, with the pace restrained until 80 paces from the enemy, when the trumpeters sounded 'Alarm!', the officers called 'Marsch!', and the whole raised their sabres over their heads. (As described in the French regulations, with sabres designed for the thrust the front rank 'pointed' their swords, only those in the rear rank raising them upright.)

There were significant differences between meeting a mounted or dismounted enemy. It was generally advocated that a charge by enemy cavalry should not be met stationary, but moving, lest the impetus of the

attacker completely overset the defender; yet there were occasions on which French cavalry in particular chose to meet a charge at the halt, with carbine-fire, though this was probably determined by circumstance. For example, at Eylau advancing Russian dragoons were mauled by a volley from the French 20e Chasseurs à Cheval before the latter engaged with the sabre; in this case the ground was so heavy with snow that the Russians could move only at a trot, giving the French more time. Such tactics were not restricted to light cavalry: a noted incident at Alteglofsheim in 1809 involved Gen Etienne Nansouty's heavy cavalry halting so that its central brigade of carabiniers could fire a volley into the onrushing Austrian heavy cavalry, before they met the charge at a trot (in the ensuing action the Austrians were defeated).

On other occasions such a tactic could result in disaster, however, as stated by the British regulations: 'Though circumstance of situation may prevent a line from advancing much, it should never absolutely stand still to receive the shock, otherwise its defeat is inevitable'.[28] De Brack nevertheless stated that awaiting a charge motionless – presumably until the very last moment, when a counter-movement would take place – could have a morale effect upon the enemy, who might be unnerved by the very stillness of their target. (He compared it to a cat stopping the attack of a dog by merely staring at it.)

Some factors were common to both infantry and cavalry engagements. Even more than in infantry combat, the maximum effect of an attack could be obtained if the enemy were struck in the flank or rear; whereas infantry could turn easily to meet the threat, controlling horses in such circumstances was extremely difficult.

Morale

As in the case of infantry close combat, morale was such a determining factor that compact bodies of cavalry in formation came into actual contact only rarely. It was more common for one side to waver before this meeting, so that the fight occurred in open order. One very experienced British cavalry officer, William Tomkinson of the 16th Light Dragoons, remarked that only once – near Fuentes de Onoro – did he know of 'two bodies of cavalry coming in opposition, and both standing, as invariably, as I have observed it, one or the other runs away'.[29] Horses will not voluntarily crash head-on into each other but will attempt to veer away, or simply pull up; one aspect of the knee-to-knee charge was that it could prevent horses from escaping to one side or the other. Commentators like Ardent du Picq stated that almost always the less determined of two opposing bodies would break a considerable time before contact was actually made, and it was on such occasions that most casualties were incurred.

Numerous commentators emphasized the morale effect exerted by an oncoming charge; de Brack, for example, advocated that swords should only be drawn shortly before contact, since the sight of this, together with the men standing in their stirrups and shouting, would both hearten the attackers and frighten the enemy. Once shaken, a body of cavalry was difficult to control, as Wellington observed in 1811:

> Few troops will bear a surprise and a general panic; and at all events young cavalry are much more easily affected by these circumstances, and the effect upon them is much more extensive and more sensibly felt… than similar circumstances operating upon infantry in the same

state of discipline. Their horses afford them means of flight, and when once cavalry lose their order it is impossible to restore it. For this reason I am always inclined to keep the cavalry out of action, as long as possible.[30]

One Austrian commentator remarked that he had never witnessed a head-to-head charge by solid formations of cavalry, but only opposing bodies exchanging blows as they moved parallel to one another. If both were compact and met head-on, he stated, the horses would touch noses and their riders would be almost unable to reach their opponents over their horses' heads, so combat would depend upon one side forcing individual mounts between those of the enemy line. (Accounts do exist of units opening their files where possible to permit the enemy to ride in, allowing both sides to slash at each other.) Thus, it was when the cavalry ceased to hold a tight formation that most combat seems to have occurred, either by the attackers losing formation in their charge, or the defenders starting to break; once this occurred, the resultant running fights could cover considerable distances, with many casualties being inflicted.

An example of the part played by morale was recalled by the cuirassier officer Aymar de Gonneville, who during the 1807 campaign engaged a body of Prussian dragoons and hussars. De Gonneville's cuirassiers were wearing

The moment of impact: this rather fanciful impression of British Life Guards smashing simultaneously into French infantry, cavalry and artillerymen at Waterloo does convey the irresistible nature of a well-timed heavy cavalry charge on already shaken troops. (Print by Bromley after Luke Clennell)

OVERLEAF Although the work of a later artist, this print from a Harry Payne painting of Life Guards charging home at Waterloo gives a convincing impression of the classic Napoleonic 'knee-to-knee' cavalry charge.

GARCIA HERNANDEZ, 23 JULY 1812

The attempt to attack squares or solid formations of steady infantry which had not been shaken in advance by artillery or volley fire was one of the most hazardous and potentially futile of cavalry actions. Techniques of attack included successive waves of cavalry, the second and subsequent waves hoping to catch the infantry as they reloaded. This could be frustrated if the infantry fired by rank, by platoons or by rolling volley, so that some element was always loaded. It was advocated that the faces of a square or solid column be attacked simultaneously, and particularly the corners where the faces met, which were thought to be especially vulnerable. Nevertheless, a resolute square was almost always secure against cavalry attack except in the most exceptional circumstances – for example, if the day were so wet that the infantry were unable to fire their muskets.

One exceptional action perhaps demonstrates the advantage of the weight of heavy cavalry. On 23 July 1812, the day after Wellington's victory at Salamanca, Gen Foy's division of French infantry was retiring along a slope when, near Garcia Hernandez, they were engaged by two brigades of British cavalry. The heavy brigade comprised the 1st and 2nd Dragoons of the King's German Legion, commanded by MajGen Baron Eberhardt von Bock, but the conduct of the action was left to the discretion of squadron commanders after Bock charged ahead with his leading squadron to pursue some French cavalry. The 2nd Squadron of 1st Dragoons KGL launched a charge against Foy's infantry under very difficult circumstances, uphill and over ground described as 'fetlock-deep in shingle'. The first French formation they encountered was in square or closed-up solid column, and this fired twice at the approaching Hanoverians, at 100 and 20 yards, causing many casualties. The leading squadron lapped around one corner of the square so that two faces were attacked at once, but the hedge of bayonets was solid – until a chance shot brought down one of the horses into the face of the square, creating a horse-length gap. Other dragoons spurred in, swinging their sabres, and from this breach the entire formation unravelled in panic. Comparatively few of the French were cut down before the remainder bolted or – mostly – surrendered, rows of muskets being laid down almost in formation.

This unprecedented success was seconded by the 3rd Squadron of 1st Dragoons, which rode against a second French square. The infantry fire was described as 'heavy and destructive', but as the dragoons approached, Frenchmen were seen to break away and run off, presumably unnerved by what had befallen the first square. Already shaken, the formation was vulnerable; the dragoons burst in just as the square collapsed, but – presumably tired by the uphill gallop – they were unable to prevent most of the French from running up the slope to join a third square. Two troops of 2nd Dragoons rode against this; again French morale collapsed, and the square broke and ran. Only when the tired and scattered dragoons came up to a steady square did the pursuit cease. General Foy (who was present) called it 'La charge la plus audacieuse de la guerre d'Espagne' ('the most audacious charge of the Peninsular War'). On the other hand, William Napier believed that it was an exception that proved the rule – that resolute infantry should never be broken, especially considering the heavy casualties suffered by the dragoons even against such shaky opposition (116 in total). The infantry on this occasion must have been tired and dispirited, and the Hanoverians especially determined. Nevertheless, whatever the special circumstances, Garcia Hernandez did demonstrate the success of an attack by heavy cavalry charging in waves.

their cloaks, so the Prussians must have believed they were dragoons from the similarity in the profile of their helmets:

> But in drawing swords, my men threw back the right side of the cloak over the shoulder, uncovering their cuirasses, and cuirassiers had a colossal reputation. So I observed a very distinct movement of hesitation in the head of the [Prussian] column; some hussars moved to the rear, and this put the troop in disorder, besides they were coming up without keeping their ranks… We came to the hussars and literally passed over them. I do not think that four of them were left on their horses, they were so overthrown by us and by each other.[31]

The effects of morale help to explain some incidents that contradicted contemporary tenets. An example from the Leipzig campaign occurred when Gen Francois-Charles d'Haugeranville's brigade of Saint-Germain's French 2nd Heavy Cavalry Division (1er and 2e Carabiniers and 1er Cuirassiers) was approached by Austrian light cavalry. Before contact was made the leading French unit (1er Carabiniers) broke and carried confusion into those following, upsetting the contemporary theory that heavy cavalry would always overpower light.

Duration

Some cavalry combat is recorded as having been of prolonged duration, but it is likely that the actual exchange of blows before one side broke and the other pursued was usually a relatively brief affair. For example, the great cavalry encounter on the plateau behind the Great Redoubt at Borodino was described as continuing for two hours, but rather than the prolonged single contest this implies, it was a continuing series of separate mêlées. Units engaged relatively briefly, then pulled away to re-organize before re-entering the fray, and increasing numbers of troops were fed in progressively.

Another noted engagement that was evidently of much shorter duration than might be imagined occurred at Venta del Pozo during the British retreat from Burgos late in 1812, in which pursuing French cavalry were engaged by Gen von Bock's 'heavy Germans' – the heavy dragoon brigade of the King's German Legion – and Gen Anson's light brigade, the latter tired from the day's earlier exertions. It was supposedly the most furious cavalry mêlée of the Peninsular War, and ended with the retreat of the British when a fresh brigade of French dragoons assailed Anson's flank; yet the actual clash was evidently momentary. Carl von Hodenberg of the 1st KGL Dragoons, who was present, wrote that:

> Our two squadrons on the right … met [the French] with such vigour that we were in an instant completely mixed – friend and foe were hardly to be distinguished. The contest, man to man, lasted perhaps a long minute, during which the ground was strewed [sic] with French, and our own loss was severe in the extreme. The two squadrons of the 2nd Dragoons did not come up quite so firm and compact as ours, so that their first shock did not do so much execution.[32]

The two German heavy regiments suffered 96 casualties, including 11 killed and 42 missing – almost a quarter of their strength.

Rallying and re-forming

It was in the immediate aftermath of a charge that a particular aspect of discipline was of paramount importance: the ability to rally and re-form. This was explained by a commentator identified only as 'W', who described how when bodies of cavalry clashed:

> one or other must either give way, turn about, and fly, or else, falling into disorder, be penetrated and passed through, so as to produce a complete mêlée, in which the party that first regains any degree of order, will have the instant advantage. This is the moment when the *arme blanche*, as the French call it [the sabre] really comes into play, and by no means in the act of charging, when the strength of the horse's legs has a far greater effect than the vigour of the rider's arm.[33]

An example of discipline in action is provided by Nansouty's division of heavy cavalry at Austerlitz in December 1805. Nansouty's command comprised six regiments: one brigade of carabiniers (at that date unarmoured) and two brigades of cuirassiers. With Gen Joseph Piston's two carabinier regiments in the lead, Nansouty charged into the cavalry of Gen Johann

A cavalry mèlée after first contact, between British dragoons and French cuirassiers at Waterloo. The fighting is realistically shown as having dissolved into contests between individuals and small groups. (Print by W. Havell after J.M. Wright)

The pursuit: troopers of the Prussian 1st Cuirassiers (Silesian) drive French infantry and gunners from the battlefield of Haynau in May 1813. (Print after Richard Knötel)

Liechtenstein's Allied 5th Column, which was posing a severe threat to the French position. The Allied first line collapsed as Gen Armand Houssaye's 2e and 3e Cuirassiers seconded the carabiniers, and Nansouty then withdrew behind the French infantry of Gen Marie-Francois Caffarelli du Falga to regroup. The remainder of Liechtenstein's column continued to threaten Caffarelli's flank, so Nansouty formed his command into 'column of platoons' (i.e. of half-companies) and passed through the gaps in the French infantry line at a trot, deploying in two lines in front of them. With the two carabinier regiments and the 2e Cuirassiers in the first line and the 3e, 9e and 12e Cuirassiers in the second, Nansouty charged again and successfully blunted the enemy threat. This was evidence of how a force of disciplined cavalry could reorganize rapidly after an engagement.

By contrast there are many examples of cavalry charges getting out of hand and careering on, sometimes to disaster, instead of rallying. Great composure was required to halt and re-form immediately after a successful charge; the natural inclination might be to pursue the beaten enemy, and indeed in some circumstances a pursuit was fully justified – but never if the troops who had made the charge were in danger of being counter-attacked. Wellington's strictures on the lack of control of the British cavalry are well known (if not entirely justified), but this was not exceptional, and even normally well-disciplined cavalry could be difficult to control in such circumstances. Although there are many examples of French cavalry rallying after one or more charges, and remaining effective and ordered even if tiring and diminishing in numbers, an instance of a cuirassier division failing to do so occurred on 16 October 1813 at Wachau, one of the actions around Leipzig.

The 1st Heavy Cavalry Division of Gen Etienne Bordessoulle, comprising one Saxon and two French brigades, was sent forward against Allied formations, and initially achieved considerable success, riding down a Russian regiment and capturing 26 guns. The Saxons consolidated their position and began to remove the captured artillery; but the French cuirassiers

The call to rally: under the eyes of Wellington's cavalry commander Lord Uxbridge (right, wearing hussar uniform), a trumpeter of British dragoons attempts to rally his regiment after their charge at Waterloo. (Print by W. Havell after J.M. Wright)

Failing to rally: in their first great charge at Waterloo men of the Union Brigade rode on to overrun the French first gun line in the haphazard manner depicted, ignoring the trumpet calls. (Print after W.B. Wollen)

The consequences of failing to rally: French cuirassiers counter-charge the disorganized Union Brigade, while lancers strike them in the flank (right). By the time the remnants regained Wellington's line the brigade had essentially been destroyed as a usable asset. (Print after H. Chartier)

charged on, apparently without being rallied and without maintaining a formed reserve. Their mounts were suffering from previous arduous service, and some of the troopers were inexperienced. Having executed their charges in column, they were unable to resist counter-charges in their flank by the Allied sovereigns' Cossack escort and by 13 Russian cuirassier squadrons. The French were hustled back and almost all the captured guns were retaken; this might not have occurred had the cuirassiers paused to re-form and reorganize before initiating any further advance.

Equally significant was the importance of maintaining a reserve in any action in which more than a very few squadrons were involved. A reserve, uncommitted in the first instance, could be crucial either for seconding a successful charge to complete the rout and pursuit of a beaten enemy, or for covering the retreat of an unsuccessful charge. Wellington explained as much in a much-quoted letter to Rowland Hill in the aftermath of the defeat at Maguilla in June 1812:

It is occasioned entirely by the trick our officers of cavalry have acquired of galloping at every thing, and their galloping back as fast as they gallop on the enemy. They never consider their situation, and never think of manoeuvring before an enemy … and when they use their arm as it ought to be used, viz., offensively, they never keep nor provide for a reserve. All cavalry should charge in two lines, of which one should be

in reserve; if obliged to charge in one line, at least one-third should be ordered beforehand to pull up, and form in second line, as soon as the charge should be given, and the enemy has broken and retired. [34]

How the charge was supposed to end, and sometimes did: French dragoons sabre broken Prussian infantry. It was during pursuits such as this that the greatest casualties were inflicted.

Wellington's summary, 1815

In the wake of Waterloo and another example of 'galloping at every thing', Wellington issued an exposition of best practice in the tactical handling of cavalry, with which most cavalry commanders of whatever nationality would have concurred. His recommendations may be summarized as follows:

The maintenance of a reserve was essential; it should not be less than half the total force and could be as much as two-thirds. Before action a cavalry force should ideally be deployed in three bodies, the first two in line and the third in column, capable of moving rapidly into line as required. When facing enemy cavalry, the first line should be 400 to 500 yards in front of the second, and the reserve a similar distance behind the second; these distances were not too great to prevent a second or third line from supporting a successful charge, nor too short to prevent a defeated first line from withdrawing without disordering those in support. Against infantry, the gap between first and second lines should be only 200 yards, enabling the second to charge before the enemy could recover his composure after firing at the first. When the first line charged, any supports should follow at a walk only, and never become carried away with enthusiasm and join the original charge: the maintenance of order was especially vital for those in support.

These instructions were intended for tactics at brigade level, but they applied equally to regimental manoeuvres.

How a misjudged charge often ended: the French *16e Dragons* are shot down by steady, unbroken Prussian infantry at Prenzlau in October 1806. Elements of two grenadier battalions were drawn up in a solid square, the front rank kneeling with 'charged' bayonets and the second and third ranks firing. They successfully repelled no fewer than seven attacks by Gen Louis-Chrétien de Bourmont's dragoon division. (Print after Richard Knötel)

Cavalry vs infantry

Different calculations were made when attacking infantry. In theory it was possible to estimate how much musketry would have to be faced according to the pace of the charge: if Adye's figures, quoted above, were correct, then if attacking cavalry began to gallop 250 yards from their target they would take about 38 seconds to reach it, during which time two volleys could be fired against them. Such calculations, however, take no account of the method of fire used by the infantry: steady troops might reserve their fire for one or more effective volleys at close range, or deliver a rolling fire over two or three ranks or by platoons. In such circumstances the attack in echelon or in column had obvious advantages, in that the leading elements would absorb the fire, in theory leaving the followers unscathed. One contemporary article on the subject stated that part of the infantry should always reserve its fire on such occasions, 'but where is the infantry which ever acted with so much countenance on the day of battle?'.[35] The same writer advocated that when attacking infantry, each wave of cavalry should be 150 yards apart, and that when attacking in line a 30-yard gap should be left between units, to permit the first waves to retire without disordering those following.

Perhaps the most difficult of the cavalry's tasks was to attack a square, against which horses would not usually charge: 'When he is urged against the terrible face of the infantry square, more resembling a living volcano than any phalanx of human invention … the animal becomes bewildered with terror, and wheeling round, in spite of rein and spur, rushes from the unequal

conflict, where he seems to know almost by instinct that his destruction is instant and inevitable'. This was described in a graphic account of the French heavy cavalry charges at Waterloo:

> Not in a single instance did they preserve their order and come in a compact body against the ridge of bayonets; and even the best of these charges ... failed at a considerable distance from the infantry. The horsemen opened out and hedged away from every volley. Sometimes they even halted and turned before they had been fired at... In this manner they flew from one square to another, receiving the fire of different squares as they passed; they flew (more frequently at a trot, however, than at a gallop) from one side of the square to another... Individuals, and small parties, here and there rode up close to the ranks. It is said that on some points they actually cut at the bayonets with their swords and fired their pistols at the officers.[36]

Under exceptional circumstances, however, squares could be penetrated, as was the case in the action illustrated in Plate H.

The frustration of heavy cavalry who have lost all momentum after being sent against unbroken infantry squares: at Waterloo 'individuals, and small parties, here and there rode up close to the ranks. It is said that on some points they actually cut at the bayonets with their swords and fired their pistols at the officers.' (Print after P. Jazet)

SELECT BIBLIOGRAPHY

English-language editions of foreign sources are listed.

Anon., *Instructions and Regulations for the Formations and Movements of the Cavalry* (London, 1801)

Anon., *Manual for Volunteer Corps of Cavalry* (London, 1803)

Ardent du Picq, C.J.J. (trans. N. Greely & R.C. Cotton), *Battle Studies* (New York, 1921)

Bismarck, F.W. von (trans. N.L. Beamish), *Lectures on the Tactics of Cavalry* (London, 1827)

Brack, A.F., *Light Cavalry Outposts* (London, 1876)

Bukhari, E., *Napoleon's Cuirassiers and Carabiniers*, Men-at-Arms 64 (London, 1977)

Bukhari, E., *Napoleon's Dragoons and Lancers*, Men-at-Arms 55 (London, 1976)

Elting, J.R., *Swords Around a Throne: Napoleon's Grande Armée* (London, 1988)

Fletcher, I., *Galloping at Everything: The British Cavalry in the Peninsular War and at Waterloo 1808–15: A Reappraisal* (Staplehurst, 1999)

Glover, R., *Peninsular Preparation: The Reform of the British Army 1795–1809* (Cambridge, 1963)

Gonneville, A.O. Le H. de (ed. C.M. Yonge), *Recollections of Colonel de Gonneville* (London, 1875)

Haythornthwaite, P.J., *British Cavalryman 1792–1815*, Warrior 8 (London, 1994)

Haythornthwaite, P.J., *Napoleonic Cavalry* (London, 2001)

Hofschröer, P., *Prussian Cavalry of the Napoleonic Wars (1) 1792–1807*, Men-at-Arms 162 (London, 1985)

Hofschröer, P., *Prussian Cavalry of the Napoleonic Wars (2) 1807–15*, Men-at-Arms 172 (London, 1986)

Hofschröer, P., *Prussian Napoleonic Tactics 1792–1815*, Elite 182 (Oxford, 2011)

Marbot, J.B.A.M. (trans. A.J. Butler), *The Memoirs of Baron de Marbot* (London, 1913)

Mitchell, J., *Thoughts on Tactics* (London, 1838)

Nafziger, G.F., *Imperial Bayonets: Tactics of the Napoleonic Battery, Battalion and Brigade as Found in Contemporary Regulations* (London,1996)

Nosworthy, B., *Battle Tactics of Napoleon and his Enemies* (London, 1995)

Pawly, R., *Napoleon's Carabiniers*, Men-at-Arms 405 (Oxford, 2005)

Rogers, H.C.B., *Napoleon's Army* (London, 1974)

Rothenberg, G.E., *Napoleon's Great Adversaries: The Archduke Charles and the Austrian Army 1792–1814* (London, 1982)

Smith, D.G., *Charge! Great Cavalry Charges of the Napoleonic Wars* (London, 2003)

Sumner, Ian, *British Colours & Standards 1747–1881 (1): Cavalry*, Elite 77 (Oxford, 2001)

Warnery, K.E. von, *Remarks on Cavalry* (London, 1798; r/p with intro by B. Nosworthy, 1997)

Wood, Sir Evelyn, *Cavalry in the Waterloo Campaign* (London, 1895)

Wood, Sir Evelyn, *Achievements of Cavalry* (London, 1897)

SOURCE NOTES

(1) *Colburn's United Service Magazine* (hereafter *CUSM)* (1844), Vol II p 439

(2) Wilson, Sir Robert, *Brief Remarks on the Character and Composition of the Russian Army* (London, 1810), pp 14–17

(3) Loyd, Lady Mary (ed.), *New Letters of Napoleon I* (New York, 1894), cccvii

(4) Wellington, 1st Duke (ed. J. Gurwood), *Dispatches of Field Marshal the Duke of Wellington* (hereafter *WD*) (London, 1834–38), Vol X p 296

(5) Capt Henry Neville, in *Journal of the Society for Army Historical Research* (1949), Vol XXVII, p 182

(6) Hay, W., (ed. Mrs. S.C.I. Wood), *Reminiscences 1808–1815 under Wellington* (London, 1901), pp 181–82

(7) *United Service Journal* (hereafter *USJ)* (1834), Vol II, pp 452–53

(8) ibid (1840), Vol III, p 370

(9) De Gonneville, Vol II, p 95

(10) *USJ* (1831), Vol II, p 61

(11) *CUSM* {1845}, Vol I, p 59

(12) Marbot, Vol I, p 300

(13) *WD*, Vol II, pp 678–79

(14) De Gonneville, Vol II, pp 99–100

(15) Beamish, N.L. (ed.), in Bismarck, Count von, *Lectures on the Tactics of Cavalry* (London, 1827), p 134

(16) *Instructions and Regulations for the Formations and Movements of the Cavalry,* (London, 1801), pp 30–31

(17) *USJ* (1829), Vol II, p 395

(18) Mercer, A.C., *Journal of the Waterloo Campaign* (Edinburgh & London, 1870), Vol I, pp 317–19

(19) Napoleon, *The Confidential Correspondence of Napoleon Bonaparte with his Brother Joseph* (London, 1855), Vol I, p 179

(20) Leach, J., *Rough Sketches of the Life of an Old Soldier* (London, 1831), pp 268–69

(21) *USJ* (1829), Vol II, pp 156–57 ·

(22) Maxwell, Sir Herbert, *The Life of Wellington* (London, 1899), Vol II, pp 138–39

(23) *CUSM* (1844), Vol II, pp 438–39

(24) Frederick II, *Military Instructions from the late King of Prussia* (London, 1818), p 137

(25) Mercer, Vol I, pp 319–21

(26) Lt Robert Winchester in Siborne, H.T., *The Waterloo Letters* (London, 1891), p 383

(27) *Instructions and Regulations...,* p 2

(28) ibid., p 34

(29) Tomkinson, W. (ed. J. Tomkinson), *The Diary of a Cavalry Officer in the Peninsula and Waterloo Campaigns* (London, 1895), p 101

(30) *WD,* Vol VII, p 277

(31) De Gonneville, Vol I, pp 69–70

(32) *Blackwood's Magazine* (March 1913), pp 300–01

(33) *USJ* (1831), Vol II, p 73

(34) *WD,* Vol IX, p 240

(35) *British Military Library or Journal* (London, 1798), Vol I, p 139

(36) *USJ* (1831), Vol II, pp 74, 463

(37) ibid, p 363

INDEX